Developing a Successful Baseball Program

Richard M. Trimble

ISBN: 1-58518-603-1
Library of Congress Catalog Card Number: 2001098602
Cover design: Jeanne Hamilton
Text design and diagrams: Jeanne Hamilton
Front cover photo: Andy Lyons/Allsport
Text photos: Richard Trimble
Illustrations: K. DeRosa (Figures 5-1, 5-2, 5-3, 5-4)

Coaches Choice
P.O. Box 1828
Monterey, CA 93942
www.coacheschoice.com

DEDICATION

To Abby

Who comes closest in the family to sharing her dad's love for The Game.

ACKNOWLEDGMENTS

There are so many people to thank who encouraged my involvement in the game of baseball. Foremost is my Dad—despite the fact that he stuck me in right field with his ratty old right-hander's mitt. It didn't dawn on him until later that his skinny eight-year-old son was a lefty.

A special thanks goes out to three other fellow coaches, because my career as a coach would not have been successful without their careful instruction and influence. My mentor was Jake Landfried at Manasquan High School. I was his assistant for 11 years, and he taught me more about the game than anyone else. Jack Hawkins runs some of the best coaching clinics in the country. If you haven't attended his *Be The Best You Are* baseball coaches' clinic held every January, you are missing an excellent opportunity to improve your coaching skills. Finally, Ernie Leta gave me a shot at coaching college baseball, and for that I'll be forever grateful.

Thanks also to Artie Gordon, John Herbert, Skip Mattola, Greg Faria, Bruce Juska, Mike Faulhaber, Pete Farnum, Ty Hawkins, Rusty Palmer, Jason Leta, Lou DeSarno, Ferris Antoon and the coaches at the Brookdale Baseball Camp, and the Lawrence brothers—Wade and "Moondog."

I would also like to recognize the athletes who posed for the photographs, all of which were taken by the author. Thanks, therefore, is extended to Joe Drew, Rick Lapinski, George Thibeault, Brad Barilla, Brenan Gordon, Andy Trimble, Luke Pearsall, T.J. Polk, Matt Mahar, Ryan DeSarno, Jeff Heckman, Chad Raub, Greg Akins, Steve Poppe, Ryan Dunn, Jeff Knight, and Andy Joseph. Additional artwork was drawn by Kate DeRosa. My typists included Jeanne Trimble, Joan Abbate, and Dick Trimble. And of course, I appreciate the efforts of my patient editor at Coaches Choice, Kristi Huelsing.

Thanks also to my wife and best friend Jeanne, who along with her late father Bill Huebner and my mother-in-law Doris Huebner, always make the game something special for me when I see them in the stands.

And then there are the players, from whom a coach learns more about the human experience than from any other source in life.

Thank you all.

TABLE OF CONTENTS

PREFACE

Although this book was intended originally for middle school baseball coaches, I found many points and plays useful for high school and Little League coaches, too. Not only does this book include 165 drills and exercises to help you develop your own coaching system, it's useful for the players themselves. Many sections can be reproduced for the players as a reference manual or playbook. Feel free to do this, and I'm honored that you've chosen to read this book.

Good luck this season.

Richard Trimble

INTRODUCTION

The purpose of this book is really quite simple: coaches who work with younger teams are coaching athletes at the single most critical juncture of their athletic careers. Yet literature addressing younger players' concerns and problems is almost nonexistent.

Why is this such a critical point in their baseball careers? For one thing, most of these boys have been playing ball since they were in first or second grade, so they've been together in Little League for at least five to six years. This is the first time they'll be trying out for a school team, and the reality of being cut from a team hits them harder as they get older. Psychological studies have shown—remarkably—that only the death of a family member outweighs the emotional trauma that an athlete feels when he's been cut from a team! Factor in the notions about peer pressure and acceptance emanating from classmates who make the team—guys they've been playing alongside with for so many seasons, growing up together—and one can sense the pressure these 12- to 14-year-olds feel.

The game itself becomes an entirely new experience for these kids as stealing, squeeze plays, and all the components of a sophisticated running game on a 90-foot diamond come into play. Pitching and cutoff systems are new. Even the proper batting swing must be taught again in many cases since the uppercut swing—which produced a fly ball homer in Little League—now only produces a fly ball that will be caught in the outfield for an out.

Adults who aren't someone's parent now coach the players. This creates new pressures as players are judged by statistical performance rather than last-name politics.

In many ways it's like starting their baseball careers all over again. But it's exciting! As coaches, you must be aware of your central role in this process, not only as teachers, but also as role models for those kids about to begin their teenage years. You must be psychologists, big brothers, disciplinarians (when needed), and field generals on the baseball diamond.

Truly, if baseball emulates life, then this level of the game epitomizes it all. Along with teaching the players' skills they'll need for high school ball, you will give them a dose of higher-level baseball realities at the same time. You're preparing them for high school life in some ways, too, as well as imparting the notion that what they contribute to their team is more important than how popular they are in school. Teaching young players commitment and a strong work ethic is vital.

This book offers an entire coaching system for youth baseball. As a varsity assistant on the high school level for over a decade, and then a head coach at a middle school for another dozen years, I drew upon systems I learned throughout my career, as well as those I developed myself. Each system is *tried and true*, but remember that every group of kids on every team you have over the years will be different and present you with new challenges.

A varsity head coach whose young son was on my team once gave me what I consider a great compliment. He told me that we did things on our middle school team that many high school varsity programs don't even do. Those words convinced me that some of my ideas for middle school might be applicable for those who coach young high school players, too, especially at the freshman and junior varsity levels.

Many of you might be surprised at the level of sophistication put into your system. You can do more things with kids at this level than you think! Whatever the level of ball your coaching, if you set lofty goals and expectations, you'll be surprised how high the kids will reach.

CHAPTER 1

The Program and
The System

Establishing a Top-Flight Baseball Program

Building a quality baseball program consists of many steps, so the following are important components needed to create a successful program.

The Coaching Staff

Baseball is too varied and complex a sport to be effectively coached with only one pair of eyes. You need at least three people to work this system and the practices described in this book, so get yourself a coaching staff, even if it means reducing your own salary in the process. It's important to hire between two and four coaches to assist you with your team. You should even consider recruiting some graduate assistants or former players who enjoy the game and are willing to volunteer their time.

Playbooks

The system in this book is sophisticated and can be confusing to young players, so it's helpful to issue a playbook such as the one included here. It describes everything they'll ever need to know in about two dozen pages. Encourage your players to read it and study it, because it may prevent a small yet costly mistake in an important game.

Your playbook should include the following:

- Cover page with a *snappy* logo
- Team rules
- Ten commandments for hitters
- Bunting fundamentals with illustrations
- Hitting fundamentals with illustrations
- Working the count as a hitter

- Working the count as a pitcher
- Batting slumps and remedies
- Call system, drop zones, and fly ball responsibilities
- Cutoff system
- Relay system
- Bunt defenses
- Rules for rundowns
- Steal reads off right-handed and left-handed pitchers
- Rules for playing the catch-up game
- First- and third-base offenses
- First- and third-base defenses
- Base running rules and reads
- Pitching mechanics with illustrations
- Pitch grips with illustrations
- Pickoff plays
- Pitching strategies
- Holding runners at all bases
- The no-cut policy and rating system explained

Make your playbook a lively read. Intersperse it with illustrative photos, diagrams, and even cartoons. Keep in mind the age and attention span of your audience.

Preseason Sweatshirts and Postseason Awards

Items like sweatshirts, hats, and awards are important for player morale. You could order hooded sweatshirts or baseball undershirts with sleeves in your team colors and hand them out to the players before the season starts. Make sure to proudly display your school name and team logo. Of course, purchasing these kinds of *incidentals* is optional, but items such as these help instill pride in the team and the entire program. Offer to sell them to parents and fans, too. It makes a great fund-raiser.

At season's end, your school probably presents some specific awards to its players. In addition to the school awards, you could give out a small plaque or trophy called the *Coaches Trophy*. This is a special award that goes to a kid who may not qualify for a school award, yet needs to be recognized for his contribution to your team. Another potential award could be an *Iron Man Award* for the player who shows up at the most practices and games throughout the season. You could even give out a jar of mustard to the biggest *hot dog* on your team!

Baseball wouldn't be baseball with the hats, so make sure your school provides a sharp looking one. If not, design one of your own and have the team buy it.

Teacher Contacts

It's important to give all the teachers in the school a copy of your roster and a game schedule, along with a memo stating that you fully support what they are doing in the classroom. Let them know that if a player needs to stay after school for extra help, then they should stay after school for extra help, preferably on practice days. Invite the teachers to the games, too. This helps to foster school spirit, and it also sends a subtle hint that you would prefer them not to hold your players after school on game days. Support classroom discipline by having the players run extra laps if they act up in the classroom.

Ceremonial First Pitch to Open the Season

A great idea for your opening season's first home game is to have your players select a teacher or school employee to throw out the ceremonial first pitch. This can be a very special moment for your school. The person selected could be a favorite teacher, a favorite secretary, a retiring custodian, a new principal, or a new president of the booster club, to name a few. The day after the game you can give this special person the ball, signed by the players.

Posting Practice Plans

The players' parents need to know exactly when their kids are expected to be on the field and when they will leave it. Grade school parents want to know this more than high school parents, so if the release time is to be delayed for any reason, post it for your players ahead of time so they can inform mom and dad.

As long as your players are well informed about practice plans and game schedules, you won't have to put up with them saying, "I didn't know I had to be there—or do that." Your practice plans should also include details like the need for players to wear covering pants if they're going to work on sliding, or if a practice is to be held indoors due to rain. You can also include conditioning plans for your players so they'll know what type of conditioning to expect after practice. And on game days, always post a copy of your lineup card.

It's important to limit practices to no more than 90 minutes of solid work—younger players have shorter attention spans. While you may run over that time frame during scrimmages, or when you'll need to keep individual players or positions for specialty training, you should generally watch the clock. High school coaches can extend this to two hours, of course.

Game Program

For your game programs, photograph each player and coach with a head and torso shot. Have each player fill out a brief profile. This should include things like their position, their grade in school, their batting average, whether they throw right or left, their jersey number, their favorite professional team, their favorite baseball moment, teachers they would most like to see at a game, and a listing of all-star or postseason honors they have won, including academic awards.

Paste the photos and profiles onto a single front-to-back sheet, or use several pages if you wish to sell ad space. (If you do choose to sell ad space, make it reasonably inexpensive and give out the game programs for free.) Create a cover logo, and add the season schedule. Make this as elaborate or as simple as you like. You can add a letter from the coaches, a listing of past championships, and so on.

If you or someone you know is good with computers, a simple layout program can help you produce a professional looking game program, instead of typing, pasting, and photocopying as needed.

Reproduce the programs in your school's copy room, fold, staple, and distribute. Hand them out to teachers, administrators, and even board of education members. Game programs are great public relations tools.

Senior Citizen Seating Area

Rope off a given area near the bleachers and offer this as free seating for local senior citizens. Have the players distribute schedules with a cover letter inviting them to home games. Remember, senior citizens often are heavily involved in budget votes that affect your school; or, they might have political connections you're not aware of. Some of them may even offer to rake the infield on game days. Most importantly, inviting the senior citizens to your games is another form of community outreach for your school.

Remembering the Best

Always save something from a championship season. A team photo or an autographed game ball will suffice. If your school has a trophy case—and most do—add this item to the collection. You might also consider creating a banner or a placard that lists the championships won by year, and putting it up in the gym, or on the outfield fence or dugout.

"Phone Home"

The first priority for coaches is understanding the kids they teach. You must pay attention to body language, facial expressions, eye contact, and even the *rumor mill*. If you ever sense anything is wrong with one of your players, try to communicate first with the child, and then with the parents if need be. As for phone calls home to parents, these can be difficult (depending on the situation), but they are necessary.

If a player is injured in a game or during practice, follow up with a call to the parents that same night. This goes far in coach/parent relationships; studies have shown that if coaches show that they care, then lawsuits are minimized.

If you ever receive a call from an irate parent, as a rule you shouldn't return that phone call for at least 24 hours. This allows for a cooling off period for the parent, and allows more time for you to prepare the proper response. Always plan out exactly how to respond to parents when they are questioning some procedure or aspect of your program or practice, even to the point of writing out notes to yourself before returning the call.

Designated Lockers

Only programs with extensive budgets and facilities can afford to give each team member his own personal locker, but there are ways to make each player feel special by having his own *place*. For example, if you have an equipment storage area that's big enough, you could build a rack or cubbyholes. Supply each player—or at least the highest-grade level of players—a spot for his name and number where he can store a spare sweatshirt, glove, batting gloves, etc. The bottom line is that this adds another element of class to the program and tells each player that he is special.

Field Day

Custodians and groundskeepers may not always share the same priorities that you have. If they just *haven't gotten around* to manicuring the field yet, and you are well into preseason, try scheduling a *field day*. It can serve as excellent bonding time for your team as well.

Bring in rakes, shovels, wheelbarrows, lawnmowers, paint, and whatever else you need to get the field in shape. Cap it off with the most important *equipment:* pizzas, sodas, doughnuts, and snacks.

Depth Chart

At the end of preseason, you should establish a *depth chart*. List every player, no matter how low on the chart (e.g., fourth-string center fielder), so that everyone knows his place in the roster. Also note that some players will be listed at several positions (but it's recommended to never be more than three positions per player). Include a depth position for pinch runners, relief pitchers, and designated or pinch hitters, too.

You should post your depth chart on the team bulletin board so that your players will have no excuse for not knowing where to report during practice. For example, you might list outfielders and infielders at different locations on the field working on different skills, or you might tell all pitchers to remain after practice. Let them know that the depth chart changes during the season as players improve in given roles and others fail to.

Holding a Youth Baseball/Softball Clinic

Invite T-ball and minor league players from local towns to your facility for a baseball clinic, and have your players act as coaches during the event. This can be one of the special highlights of your season. Figure 1-1 is an example of a clinic schedule.

YOUTH BASEBALL/SOFTBALL CLINIC SCHEDULE

8:45 – 9:05	Registration
9:05 – 9:15	Introduction/Rules/Groupings
9:15 – 11:00	Rotation through stations (15 minutes each)
11:00 –	Positional instruction. Each player chooses one of the following stations:

- Baseball pitchers – LF bullpen (form)
- Softball pitchers –CF
- Batters – cage (off machine if possible)
- Catchers – RF bullpen (all techniques)
- Outfielders – RF (sliding catch, tag-ups, rounding)
- First basemen – First base (dirtballs, relays, tag plays)
- Mid-infielders – 2B (DPs, relays)

11:25 – Wrap-up and dismissal

Figure 1-1. Youth baseball/softball clinic schedule

Set up seven instructional stations of 15 minutes each in duration (Figure 1-2). Each coach has a practice plan describing exactly what he is to teach and drill. Make it a point to cover things that parent coaches forget: sliding, form throwing, catching fly balls in the sun, etc.–things that, unless covered regularly, may lead to injuries and lawsuits. Also allow time for positional instruction in areas such as first-base play, middle-infield and outfield play, both softball and baseball pitching, and catching. Or, if the players want extra hitting, allow some of the older students to hit in the batting cage against the machine.

YOUTH BASEBALL/SOFTBALL CLINIC STATIONS AND TEACHING PLANS

Station #1: Form throwing
- Shoulder pointed at target
- Throwing from one knee and with feet planted
- Upper body rotation
- Box drill for footwork

Station #2: Hitting
- Footwork (squash the bug)
  - ✓ Weight shift and head down/in position
  - ✓ Hands held up by the ears
  - ✓ Tees and hitting stick
  - ✓ Shadow swings and side toss (coach's toss)

Station #3: Sliding
- Bent leg, pop-up, and evasive
- Tag-ups on fly balls
- Form running to first base — rounding and running through (if time allows)

Station #4: Cage hitting vs. live pitching
- Five swings and rotate

Station #5: Groundballs
- Two hands and alligators chomp
  - ✓ Paddle gloves and soccer balls for form; two hands
  - ✓ Backhanding— plant, step, whirl sequence
- Whirl sequence

Station #6: Fly balls*
- Two hands (no pan catching); fingers up
  - ✓ Ball in sun
  - ✓ Catch and crow hop

Station #7: Bunting
- Hop-turn square around
  - ✓ Pinch grip
  - ✓ Arms extended and aiming label at SS or second baseman
  - ✓ Sighting pitcher over bat handle
  - ✓ Bunt contest using targets

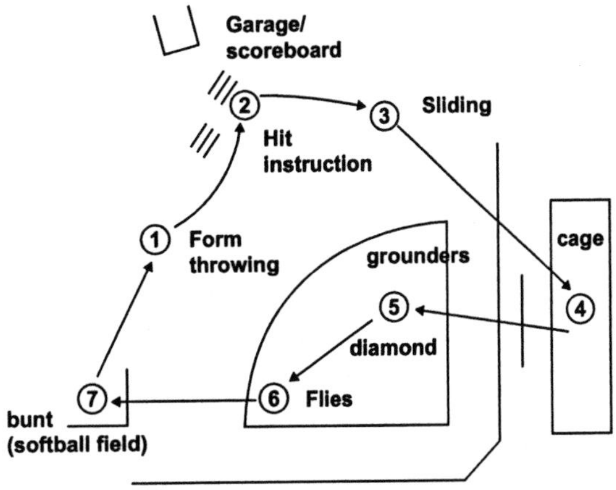

* Use a tennis ball at this station.

Figure 1-2. Youth baseball/softball clinic stations

There should be no pre-registration, so kids just show up at the door, pay about $10.00 for the 2 1/2-hour clinic, get their hand stamped, and off they go. Make sure to bring them all together to discuss safety, rules of the clinic, and how the clinic will work. Then group them together with their friends. The morning moves along quickly and it looks impressive as everyone—young and old—has fun.

All coaches should be in uniform, adding to the impression of professionalism. Make sure to share the following tips with the student coaches:

- Think safety. Envision the problems before they happen!
- Do not allow players to swing bats or throw balls without your permission and supervision.
- Notify an adult staff member immediately if a player is injured.
- Do not discipline any child yourself. Bring him to an adult staff member!
- Work, teach, and drill for the entire span of allocated time.
- Have fun with the kids!

Besides the obvious learning benefits for the registrants, it's always good for the older players to give something back to the game and the community. While their only *paycheck* is a cold soda, they do get community service hours, school merits, and so forth. You can also publicize their names in a thank you in the local newspaper.

Give the clinic registration money to your school's booster club or to the athletic fund. It is a lot of work for a modest hundred dollars or so, but the public relations benefits are enormous.

A "Special Game"

At least once every three years (so any player who plays for three years will experience this at least once), organize something special. Take the team to Cooperstown, New York, for a tour of the Baseball Hall of Fame, then play a game on Doubleday Field. If your league only plays day games, secure a field with lights and play a night game. Turn it into a community affair with lawn chairs and barbecue grills. If your community has a professional minor league team, ask if you can play a game in their stadium and sell tickets to the game. Or, hold your own all-star game. You could also organize an alumni game. Invite former players to compete with the current team. Schedule the event as a preseason scrimmage, a post-season wrap-up, or a practice game during the season. Make it a fund-raiser by selling tickets and snacks.

A Postseason Tournament

Organize a postseason tournament for teams with a .500-or-better record as of June 1. Invite all the eligible schools in your area, even if they aren't in your league. You need a minimum of three teams for the tournament. Ask each team to supply one umpire and two game balls. Secure fields with the help of the local high school, and sell tournament T-shirts to cover costs.

Selecting Team Captains

Only upperclassmen are eligible to be captains, and they must meet certain criteria. Captains need to exemplify good behavior on and off the field, especially in the classroom. Captains need to be able to communicate with the coaching staff, as they are the liaisons between the players and the coaches. Captains need to be sensitive to the underclassmen. They do not have to be the best athlete, although the kids often vote that way. Have the players vote by secret ballot. Ask each player to nominate two people. (Players may vote for themselves with one of their two votes.) The coaching staff makes the final decision. Some coaches prefer to select their own team captains without a team vote, but this system rarely works. The other team members see the captain as a *coach's pet* and often feel jealous. You can have up to three team captains, depending on the number of upperclassmen on the team. After you have announced the names of the team captains, hold a brief meeting with the captain(s). Tell them what you expect from them. Captain(s) should never discipline another player. They should bring any problems to one of the adult coaches. Put a C on your captains' jerseys to make them feel proud of their role and take it seriously.

Locker-Room Slogans and Bulltetin-Board Quotations

To inspire your team and emphasize team values, select relevant slogans or quotations and post them in the locker room and on the team bulletin board. Put up at least one new quote or slogan each week. Quotations are great teaching tools. The great Vince Lombardi reportedly watched films with General Douglas MacArthur and the latter's insights regularly peppered Lombardi's locker-room speeches. Ken Hitchcock, Stanley Cup winner and coach of the National Hockey League Dallas Stars, often uses quotes from military leaders to inspire his players. See Figure 1-3 for a list of bulletin-board quotations. Refer to Figure 1-4 for examples of locker-room slogans.

Bulletin-Board Quotations

"How you prepare is the single most important ingredient in success."—Marv Levy
"Adversity is the opportunity for heroism."—Marv Levy
"Excellence is the relentless commitment to improve."—Skip Bertman, LSU baseball coach
"Intensity plus enthusiasm equals improvement." — Coach Hubie Brown
"To win and endure, you don't have to be brilliant—just determined."—Coach Bud Grant
"Tradition never graduates."—Unknown

Figure 1-3. Bulletin-board quotations

Locker-room Slogans

(Published in *Scholastic Coach* magazine)

Anything almost right is usually wrong.

It's better to be alone than in bad company.

Don't count the days; make the days count.

Ideas don't work unless you do.

Don't go where the path leads, but to where there is no path and you can leave a trail.

The ecstasy of victory is often due to the monotony of repetition.

Success is never final and failure is never fatal.

The main ingredient in stardom is the rest of the team.

Good athletes will find a way; losers will find an excuse.

People who don't believe in miracles will never have one happen to them.

Timid athletes wait for opportunities; aggressive athletes make them.

Tough times don't last; tough people do.

Nothing great was ever achieved without enthusiasm.

—Peter Emelianchik, Reynolds Junior High School, New York, NY, 1991

No one ever drowned in sweat.

By failing to prepare yourself you are preparing to fail.

Never be willing to be second best.

Perspiration is the lather of success.

The dictionary is the only place where success comes before work.

A winner never quits and a quitter never wins.

With ordinary talent and extraordinary perseverance, all things are possible.

You are not a failure until you blame others for your mistakes.

You cannot be a failure without your own consent.

To win the game is great; to play the game is greater; to love the game is greatest.

People do not lack strength; they lack will.

Organize victory out of mistakes.

—Suzanne Blair, West Texas State University, 1984

Figure 1-4. Locker-room slogans

Showing Baseball Class

Everything you do, both on and off the field, should show players, parents, and opponents that your program is a *classy* organization. Use the following tips as guidelines for your behavior.

Umpires: Handle umpires with care. Never let the players question their calls. You can do it, but pick your battles carefully, and know when to back off. You should never get thrown out of a game.

Lineup sheets: Make up formal lineup cards on colored paper and run them off on the school copy machine. This is much classier than a scribbled lineup written on the back of a kid's school lunch bag.

Uniforms: Insist that everyone on your coaching staff wears a uniform. And insist that your kids look sharp, too. Tell them to keep their shirts tucked in, their caps on forwards, socks pulled up, etc.

Sportsmanship: Show concern for the other team and the umpires. If someone is injured, offer your services by calling first aid, getting ice, or bringing a cup of water.

Communication: Return all phone calls and call in game scores promptly. Respond to any and all press inquiries. If asked about the opponent, always praise them or someone on their team. Never blame a loss on the umpires or your team's failure; praise the opposition instead.

Game scores: Never run up the score, even if the opposing coach did it to you. Take off the running game and do not bunt to bring in runs or advance players if you are ahead by several runs late in a game. Substitute freely and experiment with new players in new positions. If the baseball game begins to show a football score, turn off the scoreboard.

Cleanliness: Keep the equipment area and the clubhouse clean and neat. Clean up the bench area after every game, home and away.

Discipline: Never use foul language in front of your players. Do not single out a player in the midst of a game to scream at him for an error. Instead, talk to him alone on the sideline at the end of the inning. This is more discreet, and more effective, too. However, if your player does something that is highly visible and totally lacking in class (such as yelling at an umpire or coach, cursing so that everyone can hear, or even defying you from out in the field), do not hesitate to pull him out of the game immediately. Parents, administrators, and other players expect you to address inappropriate behavior.

Pregame routine: Before the game begins, welcome the opposing coach with a handshake and give him your lineup card. Congratulate him on a recent victory or ask him about a team he's already played. The other coach will value the fact that you respect his opinion, and you can learn a thing or two about an upcoming opponent. If you're playing at home, make sure the opponent gets a game ball right away, to give their pitcher plenty of time to warm up before the first pitch. If you're scrimmaging with another team, let them use the batting cage during the workout. Don't forget to go over the ground rules with the captains of both teams before the game or scrimmage begins.

Postgame routine: After a game, have the players line up at home plate to shake the opponents' hands and congratulate them on a good game, or, if it was a blowout victory for your team, to thank them for coming and wish them good luck the rest of the season. You should go directly to the opposing coach and say something of a similar nature to him. If he has a big game coming up, wish him luck. If you have won handily, pick out one of his players who performed well and mention how great he did. If the opposing pitcher threw a great game against you or an opposing hitter crushed a home run against you, give him the game ball.

Fund-Raising Ideas

Sometimes, you will want to buy things for your team that aren't in your budget. You can cover these expenses with periodic fund-raising activities, but avoid tapping the community chest too often, or it becomes overkill.

Two of the simplest ways to raise money—publishing a game program with ads and offering a Little League instructional clinic—were described earlier in this chapter. You can also try some of the following ideas:

- Refreshment sales at home games
- Car wash
- Bake sale
- Rummage/Garage sale
- Golf outing (This can be very lucrative, but consult someone who knows how to run a golf fund-raiser because it takes some expertise and contacts.)
- Raffle (Use donated prizes such as professional game tickets, etc.)
- Souvenir sales, such as hats, T-shirts and sweatshirts. Always consider the financial outlay versus the potential profit.

Keep accurate records of all fund-raising activities. Coaches have lost their jobs over questionable financial practices regarding independent moneys. Don't forget to support fund-raising programs by other teams. If you hear that they are selling something or soliciting funds for a special purpose, buy the item or send them a modest check on behalf of your team.

Personal Priorities

To help your team be successful, you need to set coaching priorities for yourself. Your first priority should be personnel assessment. You need to fit each and every player into a position (or two or even three) where he can be his best and contribute most to the team. You also need to think about what kind of system you will need to install, based on your personnel. Although this is less important in baseball than in other sports, such as football or ice hockey, you must always fit your system to the kids, never the other way around. For example, if you have no power, but you have good team speed, then you need to stress an aggressive running attack.

Your second priority should be personal knowledge. Are you continually updating and enhancing your knowledge of the game? Do you read books and articles, go to clinics, and query other coaches? Never be satisfied with what you know, because what you don't know may beat you. Have you read the rule book? You should. Highlight and underline the most important sections.

Your third priority is getting organized. Make sure your practice time and your overall program are organized. In the words of Pat Riley, "Winning is the science of preparation, and preparation can be defined in three words: leave nothing undone. No task is too large. The difference between winning and losing, success and failure, can be the smallest detail."

Putting together a game plan for every game should be your fourth priority. Scout opponents so you'll know how to attack them and how to defend against them. Prepare your team for anything that might happen—everything from who hits where, to who bunts, and who steals.

Ask of yourself what you ask of your players. Anything less from either side can spell defeat. Your goal as a coach at this level is to be the best coach your team has ever played for. They may play for better coaches down the road, but for right now, you want to be the best they have ever seen in this sport.

Motivation

Youth players have attention spans roughly equal to an MTV video. That will not sustain them through a seven-inning game. One of the key factors in successful coaching at this level is motivation. You need to constantly work to motivate your players, to set a theme, and to keep the kids focused.

Give your practices a motivational focus and post it with the practice plan. You can make it general (for example, "We need to have a great practice today.") or specific (for example, instead of a regular batting practice, run players through hitting stations labeled *Driving the middle* and *Suicide-squeeze bunting.*). Inspire your team by filling the team bulletin board with exciting game photos (such as a player sliding headfirst into second amid a cloud of obscuring dust), motivational quotes (as discussed earlier in this chapter), and coaching tips. When the season gets underway, post news clippings about the other teams in your league.

Communicating with your players is also important. Start every practice with a quick statement of the goals for that practice session. After practice, do not dismiss players from the field without a final team roundup. Prepare your comments in advance, and cover one or two key points. Pregame briefings are especially important. Always review the signs, your game plan, and perhaps something from the scouting report. Stress the importance of the game. If the game is a big one and the kids know it, crack a joke to relieve their tension. Never send them out on the field without fine-tuning their focus.

Periodic team roundups during the game are essential too. Use these sparingly and wisely, however, or they will become a cliché. Say things like, "We are playing for one run here, so check your signs," or "This pitcher's got slow speed. You are over-swinging," to help your players refocus. Always end these meetings with a team handclasp and shout a keyword such as *win* or *think* or your team name.

Be careful how you communicate with your players. When your team wins, use the term *you*, and when your team loses, say *we*. If you have reprimanded a player during a practice or in a game, find something to praise him for before he leaves the playing field.

In addition to motivating your team as a whole, you need to motivate each individual player. One-on-one meetings are an effective way to do this. Sit down with each player that's having a problem and explain why they need to step up their play or become more team oriented, or what they need to do to improve their game. Doing this in front of the entire ball club is almost never appropriate. Furthermore, do not be afraid to lay it on the line in a quiet one-on-one meeting with such challenges as "last year you hit .233......I can't play you this year if your average stays there" or "how well you pitch as the number two pitcher will go far toward determining how successful we are this season as a team."

Discipline

George S. Patton once commented, "With discipline, you are irresistible." But remember, discipline has many different components. It ranges from the self-discipline you need as a coach; to attend clinics and work at improving even when other responsibilities may be more attractive. Discipline then moves into the realm of *team discipline* as reflected in proper uniform attire, crisp infield drills, and sharply orchestrated practices. And finally, it includes that most undesirable aspect – disciplining kids who break the rules.

Here are several rules to apply to yourself as the disciplining coach:

BE FLEXIBLE—Written team rules need not bind you since you have to see them as *the end of the rope*. There is always slack in the rope before you need to hang yourself, or your players, with it. Be patient and avoid emotion. Know all the facts before you serve as the judge, and ultimately, the jury.

TAKE YOUR TIME—*Do not rush to judgment*, but rather, secure as many facts and opinions as you can within a reasonable amount of time. Sort out what is valid and what is hearsay. Read between the lines and weed out private agendas, stretched *truths*, and cover-ups.

TAKE EACH INCIDENT CASE-BY-CASE—Make sure you have secured all the facts and background in any discipline case. (Bear in mind that you need only contact witnesses, participants, and staffers—you don't need to call everyone, especially those who were not present or may engage in lies to cover themselves and therefore cloud the issue.) Examine why the child did what he did. Are there extenuating circumstances such as family crises (a divorce, a death) classroom pressures, or personal issues? Is the troublemaker a first-time offender or is he a repeat offender? Weigh such factors in your decision.

DON'T AIR DIRTY LAUNDRY—Unless you can impart a team lesson, you shouldn't involve your entire team in individual disciplinary matters. Keep the facts to yourself and the adjudication within your staff. Seek input from the coaching staff as to the rectitude of your decision, too, as you need to maintain a common front and *be on the same page*. There will be times, however, when you can use a bad situation to your benefit. For example, "John has been dismissed from the team because—" can be a valuable lesson for the team as to how far you can be pushed.

Also, make the tough calls yourself. If the majority of the coaches disagree with you, then you may need to prioritize and re-consider. But if you feel strongly about a certain matter, then make the call alone. You do the disciplining as the head coach. Do not pass off the heavy matters to an assistant coach. You will want to handle the disciplinary action yourself so that you know exactly what transpired in case you are challenged on the matter. By removing disciplinary action from your assistants, this allows them to be closer to the kids, thus creating a healthy *buffer zone*. It also relieves them of the disciplining burden, which is not an enjoyable one. You never want to create an *us vs. them* atmosphere on the team between coaches and players. You handle the big issues and let the assistant coaches be the players' allies.

Remember that we are all teachers before we are coaches. Although disciplinary actions are never fun, they are necessary for the education of the player. Even if the kid is your number-three hitter and top pitcher, he must be taught that he is not above the law. Do keep in mind that these are kids before they are baseball players, but they must understand that society has boundaries. Also, a mistake made on a middle school team that leads to their dismissal from the squad is far less injurious at this point in their careers than it will be when they are playing varsity in high school, and perhaps being scouted by colleges. If you teach them a disciplinary lesson now, it may be more helpful to their future development than any correction of their batting stance will ever be.

Handling Parents

You are probably well aware of the horror stories when it comes to dealing with angry parents, but there are things you can do to help limit these. For one, the *no cut policy* is a savior, and second, running a B-team helps alleviate many confrontational situations. Third, since all coaches should be very concerned about keeping accurate statistics and records, as well as publishing them in newsletters, you should have the data on hand with which to justify your personnel moves. Baseball is the easiest sport to validate as game and player statistics abound as your evidence. For example, John is playing because he is hitting .408, while former Little League All-star Billy is not playing because he is hitting .235, with six errors in the field. Know your numbers; use your numbers. It would also behoove you to invite parents to an orientation after one of your early preseason practices. The nature of the meeting is essentially a question and answer session.

You should give out your home telephone numbers to your players and their parents. You should also return every single phone call—but sometimes, if the situation is volatile—you should apply the *24-Hour Rule* as described previously.

You should never let a parent walk out onto your practice field, yell and scream because they're unhappy about something, and disrupt your workout. If you ever feel that a confrontation is looming, call the parent to set up a private meeting after practice. You may need the presence of your assistant coaches or even a school administrator to prevent a *he said/she said* situation later.

Be prepared for your meeting and never let emotion cloud your judgment. Offer specific suggestions for improving the performance of the child in question. Try to see yourself as a doctor meeting with a sick patient, "here is what I recommend they do to get better." Always exhibit cool but caring professionalism.

If you have been fair as a coach, your reputation will precede you. Rely upon the collective judgment of your coaching staff, as well as the reputation you have established, to bolster your confidence. Remember that you are seeing the player's performance day in and day out, in practice as well as games. The parent might only see the games, so obviously your assessment of the player's abilities will be more rounded. Also, keep records of attendance, as this can be helpful in defending your personnel moves.

Some coaches prefer to keep all practices closed to parents. You may choose to do this, but you also might want to demonstrate the sophistication of your program, your practice, and your organization. Again, always conduct yourself with an air of polite professionalism, and never discuss another player's misdeeds or faults with a parent. Your staff handles personnel moves in-house.

There will be times when you explode on a player during practice, but never do so during a game unless it is discreetly off to the side and with your arm around the player. Think about this—if a parent sees you with your arm around his son, he cannot tell if you are reprimanding him or coddling him. This does not mean that you can't yell at your team as a whole during a game. Collective chastisement is seen as *tough love* coaching while singular, verbal discipline is seen as *picking on my son*. There is never a need to publicly embarrass any player. A parent has a legitimate gripe if you do so.

Keep your stats and keep your cool. Your parent conferences will be kept to a minimum if you do so. Be confident in the job you are doing and in your sense of fairness.

The Written Word

Written communication is vital to effectively integrate your team into the school community, keep the school teaching and administrative staff on your side, and to keep players, coaches, and parents informed as to what is going on.

Your baseball bulletin board should be a focal point of interest throughout the season. You should insist that the players consult the board every single day. On it will be posted the daily practice plan, announcements, copies of the newsletters, and a visual learning section entitled *Improve Yourself*. This visual learning section offers tips and coaching points, usually accompanied by a photo or diagram on things like hitting, position play, or the mental aspect of the game. Copies of the daily practice plan should also be distributed to the coaches' mailboxes each morning.

Newsletters are invaluable in keeping communication open between your coaching staff, your players, their parents, school administrators, and the community at large. Newsletters can contain announcements (such as school or booster club functions that relate to baseball), statistics, schedule changes, a section called *Player of the Week*, and game results. Newsletters should be published approximately once a week, and are given to the players, coaches, school staff, and hopefully, brought home to the parents. Keep spare copies on file, because they make for an easy end-of-season report to the school administration should your school require one.

Whenever you win a game, a brief announcement should be made during the morning school address. This tells the school the score of your game and the highlights. One paragraph is all that is necessary. You should save these and put them right into the newsletters in the game results section rather than having to re-invent the wheel.

By the way, be prudent in your selection of *Player of the Week*. Try not to name the same player over and over again. It's important to mention as many players as you can at least once during the season, although this is not politically motivated and the athlete must do something to warrant it. If an underclassman is to be cited for extraordinary accomplishment, fine, if a non-playing upperclassman never gets cited, that's okay, too.

Team Rules

Opinions vary as to the necessity and validity of providing written rules and regulations. Some coaches prefer not to lock themselves in by having published team rules, but written rules eliminate gray areas and make things crystal clear which is especially important for younger players. Team rules should be sent home with every player for their parents to examine, too. Some teams ask that the parents sign the team rules as an acknowledgment of receipt, but that is up to you.

The following is an example of *Team Rules*. They should be given out during your first team meeting and included in your playbook.

- No drinking, smoking, and drugs are permitted. Expulsion from the team is automatic and without appeal. Chewing tobacco is also not permitted.

- You must maintain regular, good academic standing. Every one of your teachers will be contacted and your work/behavior in the classroom will be monitored.

- Lateness to any practice or game means the running of a *mile*. No excuses – just run. Lateness to an away game means that you have missed the bus and you will not play (do not try to get there by your own means). Lateness for a home game means that you will not start the game.

- Missing practice will not be tolerated. If you are absent from school, or if you have put a note explaining your absence in the coach's mailbox BEFORE PRACTICE, then you will be excused providing the reason is acceptable. An unexcused absence is considered a *cut* and is punished with the running of a mile; a second *cut* and you are dismissed from the team. If you miss practice, excused or otherwise, on the day before a game, you will not start that game.

- Any player will be allowed to remain in class for extra help from a teacher. You must bring a note from that teacher in order to be admitted late without running penalties. You should see your teachers for extra help on practice days rather than on game days.

- Sunday batting practices are optional (always held prior to Monday games). Honor your family commitments first.

- Vacation practice sessions are considered optional ONLY if you are going away with family. Otherwise, you are expected to report to practice.

- If a teacher contacts the coaching staff about you not doing your homework, or misbehaving in class, you can expect to run a mile for it. Conversely, if you receive an A-grade on a test, quiz, or a paper, we will reward you with reduced running. The coaches must have a note or see the actual paper/test/quiz.

- Uniforms should always be clean and properly worn—sox, hat, shirt tucked in, hose, etc. Look sharp and you play sharp. You represent the team, the school, and your family.

- You will not cut down another player or coach: you are part of a team. You will play for this team, not yourself. If you are having a problem with a teammate, see your coach or your captain(s).

- KNOW WHAT'S GOING ON AT ALL TIMES. Always check the baseball bulletin board every day, because there might be something new put up like practice plans or announcements or updated stats.

- In choosing to come out for this baseball team you are asked to prioritize this program over others you may be playing for. Little League, travel soccer, school plays, after-school jobs, etc., must be considered secondary. We will try to accommodate your other interests, but not at the expense of this team. Little Leaguers are allowed to attend a game in lieu of our practice, but they will be dismissed no earlier than one-half hour before game time.

- No pitcher is allowed to throw for any other team (Little League, Babe Ruth, etc.) during the season without checking with the coaching staff first.

No-Cut Policy and Rating System

After a month of preseason evaluation, your coaching staff should rate each player and assign a ranking number to them. Usually, only the top 10 players get the majority of the playing time in varsity games, because it is important to build a winning team and potentially win a divisional title. These top 10 players are not necessarily ranked 1-10, but rather, they are collectively grouped (i.e.—no one can say they are *The Best*).

The next set of numbered players, 11 to 15, should see spot action in specialized roles as pinch hitters, defensive replacements, and pinch runners. They, and every player beneath them in the rankings, will play on the B-Team on as consistent a basis as possible. It's unrealistic to seek equal playing for all players on the B-Team in each game. Every player, varsity or B-Team, should be given a uniform and full recognition in status as a member of your baseball team. They should be able to earn jackets and trophies just like everyone else in the program as you all practice together, work together, and win or lose together.

Keep in mind that if a player wishes to drop off because of a low ranking, this is his prerogative, but you should ask that he come to you to discuss his decision. The bottom-ranked players are just not listed in the qualitative order (i.e. – no one can say that they are the worst). You should publish weekly stats and as the season progresses and players improve or slump, members of your team will be moved up or down on the depth chart. Only the depth chart is posted, so every player must know his role as you work toward a common goal: winning.

A no-cut policy will probably be the most innovative component of your program and should be written in *stone*. When your numbers are big, it will result in fewer at bats, practice fungoes, and so forth, and it may mean that your team is less prepared going into the season, but it is a fair trade-off. It means that you should lengthen your practices, run your players a little harder to see who really wants to play, and bring in specialized positional groups. You may want to run extra and optional batting practices for those in need of improvement.

On the other hand, think things out and be sure that every one of the older players, even if their rating is low, has some sort of specialized role on your team – make them scorekeepers, have them draft pitching charts, teach them to read the opposing team's signs, have them help run the bullpen, etc. Give a non-starter the honor of stealing the 100th base of the season, or use them as a pinch runner on suicide-squeeze plays where intelligence counts as much as speed. Use them as bunters in key situations or designated runners for pitchers and catchers coming off the bases with two outs under the *speed-up* rule. Find something that they can hang their hat on and know within themselves that they have contributed.

Do you need extra coaches to make this system work? Absolutely. If you can enlist graduate assistants, that's great, but every year you should take a portion of your salary and give it out to your extra coaches no matter how big or small your ball club is.

Can this system work if the number of players trying out for your team is excessive, perhaps even in the 70-to-80-player range? Yes, you could still try to make it work. You should only allow seventh and eighth graders to try out than allowing sixth graders— they still have Little League as an alternative. But even if your number remained high, you could have a C-Team. Do what you can, but it is advised to not cut kids at this age.

Is this no-cut policy something to be used on the high school level? Perhaps on the freshman teams, but once the player reaches junior varsity, and certainly varsity level, the reality of their limitations must set in. More often than not, the kids will weed themselves out as they sit on the bench, but the idea that high school varsity is as high as most baseball players ever rise actually justifies cutting those whose talents simply do not allow them to play at this level.

But remember—the world can be cruelly competitive, and although it is important to expose your players to this, you can ease them into it and shelter them a little longer. Back in Little League and recreational ball, every child should have had the chance to play in every game. But when they reach high school, they will face the reality that they may not be good enough to ever play again. Middle school baseball can serve as the transition, so you need to be sensitive to how easy or difficult you can make that transition.

Meetings

Meetings are an essential part of your baseball program for keeping the lines of communication open. You should begin with a *preseason coaches meeting* to get the thoughts and feelings of your staff about the upcoming season. This includes putting everyone on the same page systemically as well as going over changes in what you may wish to teach during the upcoming season. It's always important to discuss new ideas, techniques, and plays you plan to infuse and implement.

You should hold a *sign-up meeting* to be held well before the opening day of preseason. Make sure that your meeting does not conflict with the in-season sports at the time. For example, basketball coaches may be a little miffed if you get their players thinking baseball during a basketball playoff run. This is understandable; be sensitive to it. At the sign-up meeting, have the player candidates fill out a 3" x 5" card with their name, address, home phone, grade, positions played, and positions preferred. Also, have them write down their batting and throwing hand (R/L), and make sure you have their parents' last name if it is different than their own. Explain your program, team rules, and starting date. Remind them of such obligations as physical exams and release forms, running to get in shape, and so forth. The handout containing all of this information from the first meeting can be easily given to players who may not be able to make that meeting. It is important to put everything in writing.

Once your preseason is finished, then you should have an equally important coaching meeting called the ratings meeting. As explained previously, you should rank and rate each player to inform them of how much playing time they can expect. Each coach is given a copy of the preseason stats and roster. The player cards from the first meeting are kept on hand, too. Each coach will assess each player on a 1-2-3 basis. Players rated as 1 are the starters—even blue chippers if you have some. The 2's are borderline players, and will most likely see some playing time. The players at the 3 level are definitely B-Team players. Now, discuss these ratings with your staff, decide who are the top ten (i.e., varsity players) and set up your depth chart at this point. The cards the players had filled out may be helpful in placing a B-Team player somewhere on the depth chart. This is essential – every player must be assigned a spot on the depth chart.

Once you've had the ratings meeting, you should then hold individual meetings with every player. You could have your assistant coaches handle practice while you meet with every athlete. The player should be explained his ranking and position on the depth chart, as well as expectations for personal improvement. Emphasize that the depth chart, which is posted (ratings are not posted), is changeable. There will always be mobility as players improve or slump.

Pitcher and catcher meetings need to be held periodically. Late in the preseason you should hold a meeting to discuss pitching strategies on how to get a hitter out. You should also have a brief meeting with the pitchers at the beginning of each game to go over the rotation for that week.

Similar to the pitcher meetings, you should always meet briefly with your key players and captains to assess team attitudes and concerns, make suggestions to help their hitting or fielding, and so on. The lines of communication need to be kept open at all times. Why not jog with certain players during the Monday Mile and turn that into an individual meeting? It's good for team morale, and it's good for you!

Mound conferences during games qualify as *meetings*, too—and these are some of the most critical. Remember that pitchers are *in the spotlight* and under considerable pressure. High school rules limit you to one conference per inning, and three overall. Exceed that and the pitcher must be removed, so it's vital to use your conferences wisely.

If the pitcher is in a *negative groove* where he has trouble finding the plate, signal the catcher to go out and talk with him. What you talk about is unimportant; the fact that you are interrupting the negative groove is. If that doesn't work, then you need to go out to talk to the pitcher. Be positive and calming. Yelling at the pitcher rarely works. Remind him to concentrate on the glove and his mechanics. He may be upset at the umpire's calls. Remind him of what the umpire is calling and have him work to hit the proper zone. Remind him to throw strikes and rely on his defense, or remind him of the aiming points on the breaking pitch. If you have a big lead late in the game and the pitcher gets too *cocky* and begins walking people, remind him that walks allow a team back into the game – he has to throw strikes. Even the best hitters will fail to hit the ball safely 70% of the time.

You should always begin the season with a *fun meeting,* such as a barbecue. Have each player assigned an item such as soda or chips; you can provide the hot dogs, the grill, the culinary expertise, and some inspirational video clips. The clips are taken directly from previous highlight films and from the final at bat in the movie "The Natural." This meeting is always a fun time and tends to put the season ahead in perspective and align your thinking.

As stated previously, it is important to call a *parents meeting* on the eve of the season. Introduce yourself, your staff, and your goals. Discuss playing time, philosophies about winning, losing, learning, and discipline. Then make time for a question and answer period.

You should always wrap up your season with a *player improvement meeting*. You should review individual stats, team stats, and a program for improvement in the off-season. Suggest what position they might be playing next season. These individual meetings should take only about five minutes each, but they bring a sense of closure to the finished season and an introduction for the next one.

Scouting

You should always scout your next opponent. You will feel much better if you have seen the other team play before you play them. If you can't go to an opponent's game personally, send one of your assistant coaches.

While scouting a future opponent's team, you or one of your coaches should:

- Take a photocopied page from the score book and indicate where the opposition batters hit the ball. Make sure they draw in the lines where a single or double went.
- Observe how good the catcher's arm is. Can your team steal on him?
- Observe what kind of double steal offenses and defenses they use.
- Observe who steal bases for them, and if they go on the first or the second pitch.
- Observe who their pitches are and what each one throws. How are their moves to first? Where do they try to locate the pitches? How is their velocity? Is there a pattern to their pitching?
- Observe whether or not you can run on the outfielder's arms. If so, which ones?
- Observe who their good bunters are and where they place the ball. Do they use the squeeze play?
- Observe if they run any pick-off plays.
- Try to decipher the coaches' signs.
- Observe what kind of discipline their team exhibits.
- Observe what kind of cut-off system they use.
- Observe how deep their backstop is if you will be playing on their field.
- Observe what their fans are like? (You will need to warn your team if their fans are rowdy and distracting.)
- Observe if any of their hitters chase wild pitches.

You should feel more confident playing a team you have scouted. The mere placement of your defense against their hitters alone will be invaluable.

If you have not been able to scout your opponent in a previous game, at least assign one coach to watch their pregame. Look for error-prone infielders, weak outfield arms, and the strength of the catcher's arm. If you have enough coaches, assign another to watch the pitcher warm up. See what he is throwing and how serious he is about his pitching. Is he struggling with the catcher to get a particular pitch? What is his delivery from the stretch? Does he have a high-leg kick or does he slide step? No need to overtly act like a spy; merely observe with intent.

The game itself produces a scouting report. You should ask your scorekeepers to record the location of base hits. After the first time through the batting order, request data from you're your scorekeepers such as "did this guy steal the last time," or "where did he hit the last time up?" This way you can alert your outfielders and/or re-align your defense accordingly. After the game you should jot down some notes about systems play, weaknesses, strengths, flaws, first and third, bunt coverage, etc. It only takes a few minutes to write this information down, and it will reap you dividends the next time you play that opponent.

The B-Team

The B-Team is an important component to your ball club. Playing your starters against your B-Team in practice will improve every player's performance, and your team's performance. While it's important to note that you can't play every player in league competition, your B-Team can have a mini-league of its own. The B-Team schedule is usually abbreviated depending on other teams who are willing to arrange B-Team contests.

The benefits of B-Team games are numerous:

- You can develop younger and lesser-skilled players for future varsity play.

- You can introduce your starters to other positions and this can benefit their future careers and your team.

- You can work with players who normally do not get enough repetitions in the course of a busy practice week because your emphasis in on the varsity starters.

- If a player gets hot and goes three for three at bat in a B-game, then you have discovered someone to bring up for a varsity look.

- You can work your relief pitchers who may have been inactive during the game week.

- In the sense of fair play, you have avoided cutting the lesser-skilled players, yet you have provided them with opportunity to show their skills (or lack of them) to parents who may be suspicious of your evaluation of their child's talents.

Since B-Team games can be marathons, you should pre-arrange a two-hour time limit (or six innings, whichever comes first) with the opposition coach. You should also agree to an unlimited substitution rule. Enter and re-enter players at will. You could align your entire roster in one batting order with multiple designated hitters so that every kid gets between one and three at bats. You could set up a rotation whereby players switch in and out of positions on their own during the course of the game. See that every kid plays. You might try to guarantee two innings in the field and one at bat for each player. The exceptions would be your varsity players who are hitting well enough so that they do not need to work in this regard, and they will only play the field in a position where their skills are being tested and developed.

Enjoy the "Killer B's," because there is absolutely no pressure to win. You should always go out to a local fast food restaurant for a B-Team luncheon after your last away game.

If funding such a B-Team arrangement is a problem, there is a simple set of solutions to help facilitate your B-Team league. Parents can drive the players to away games and coaches can umpire the game from behind the mound. No cost and no cuts—there are few, if any down sides to playing a B-Team schedule. It makes for an enjoyable Saturday morning.

Practice Organization

Effective coaching—like anything in life—begins with having a plan. This is one of three central rules in orchestrating a good practice. The other two rules are timing and station work.

When planning practices, remember to schedule time for each of the skills and rules listed in Figure 1-5. Everything listed will be covered in detail later in this book. You'll also need a daily practice plan (like the one in Figure 1-6) – written out and posted for the kids to see. Block your time frames into roughly 20-minute segments and keep to the clock. For an athlete, nothing is more monotonous than a seemingly endless and boring practice. Inform your kids what time they can expect to be off the field and then stick to it. Parents concerned with pick-up times and dinner hour will appreciate this, too. Keep the players moving and keep in mind adolescent attention spans.

Station work will facilitate a better teaching atmosphere, with more kids actually working at any given time during the practice. For example, if you are still doing the old batting practice where a coach or a player tries to find the plate pitching to a solitary batter and where all of the other kids stand around for an hour, then you are doing a disservice to your team, and to the game. All too often kids leave baseball because it is *boring*, and this style of baseball is boredom personified.

Set up your stations. One group may work off the batting tee while another works the ball-toss drill off the screen. Another hits off a pitching machine or live pitching in a batting cage. You may be saying at this point, we do not have a pitching machine and/or batting cages. This should not be used as an excuse to fall back into the old stand-around-batting-practice. Have one group work on bunting or have a coach hit fungoes out to selected fielders at their defensive positions in between pitches. Divide your team into positional groups such as infielders and pitchers/catchers. Allow one station in your rotation to be a defensive on in which your are, for example, working the infielders in relay/cutoff techniques, charging slow rollers, and working backhand pick ups. The other two groups will hit. Then, when the outfielders show up in the rotation, they see fly balls in the gaps, grounders in a rounding drill, and sliding-catch techniques. Each station need only be 20 minutes in length, so the groups will hit for a total of 40 minutes and work defense for 20 minutes in a one-hour block of the time set aside for these stations.

Even when teaching basic skills such as hitting, call the team together for a group demonstration and then follow that up with stations emphasizing such isolated techniques as the downward approach with the front arm, the back-heel roll, and high

---

BASEBALL: SEASONAL CHECKLIST   YEAR:_____

FUNDAMENTALS: OFFENSE:
___throwing form   ___sliding
___hitting   ___running to 1b
___fielding   ___leads
___bunting   ___running rules
___*crow hop*   ___bunt-run offense
                                       ___suicide squeeze
TEAM PLAY AND PHILOSOPHY: ___double suicide
___teacher contacts   ___1-3 offense
___play book   ___*2-play* off 1-3
___team rules   ___fake bunt/hit
___hitting rules   ___hit – n – run
   ___opposite field hitting   ___automatic/normal off 2b
   ___curveball rule   ___automatic/normal off 2b
   ___belt high FB   ___leads-reads-steal: RHP
   ___take   ___leads-reads-steal: LHP
___Green Light Rule   ___backstop rule: read or reaction
___signs
___base running signs
___Ted Williams' count theory
___catch up game

MISCELLANEOUS:
___pepper
___lefty drag bunting
___righty push bunt

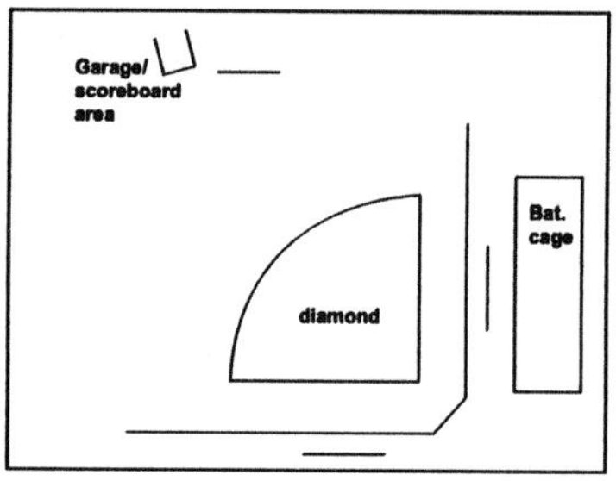

Figure 1-5. Season checklist

follow through off three separate batting tees. These stations can be as brief as five to seven minutes while each kid gets five to ten repetitions.

Remember that players are the freshest when you first see them, so after stretching, throwing, and agilities, you should go right into a team function or systems play such as first and third offenses, bunt defenses or base-running rules, all of which are taught and then drilled or practiced. This lasts for perhaps 20 to 25 minutes and then you should go into the type of batting practice station-work described previously. (It is imperative that baseball players hit every day, so batting practice, however you choose to run it, is an integral part of each practice, even when indoors.) You can finish up with conditioning or perhaps situation simulation.

Practices should usually last 90 to 120 minutes, but no more. If indoors, you may go 75 to 90 minutes, but no less. The kids go home having been worked hard and having learned something new in every practice.

PITCHING:	OTHER POSITIONAL DEFENSIVE SKILLS:
___pitch grip	___catchers: framing
___types of pitches	___foot work and throwing form
___pitching charts	___giving signs
___post game arm care	___pop fouls
___covering 1b	___applying tags
___holding runners	___OF: depths (20' rule)
___check call	___vs. tag ups
___pitching form	___vs. fence
___pickoffs	___sliding catch
___0-2 pitch	___rounding
___1-3 strike rule	___do or die play
___change up	___ IF: snap throws
___2 types of FB	___charging slow rollers
___pitchouts	___backhanding
	___short hops
	___fly balls in sun
DEFENSE:	
___call areas/drop zones	___relay techniques
___call system	___speed throw
___cut off and backups	___DP pivots
___relay system	___bunt defense
___pick off plays	___1b-man's play
___run-downs	___40-60/46-64: holding R-2
___1-3 defenses	___infield depths

Figure 1-5. Season checklist (cont'd)

```
DAILY PRACTICE PLAN

                        __/__/  M  T  W  T  F  ST

DAY ONE
Be on field at 3:05 pm ready to go!
Dress warmly: bring an extra sweatshirt


3:05 – 3:40 stretching routine and throwing
3:40 – BATTING FUNDAMENTALS from the waist down
3:50 – Station work:  hit–n–stick
                      T's
                      Short toss in cage
                      5 minutes at toss machine
4:10 – BATTING FUNDAMENTALS from the waist up
4:20 – stations again 5 minutes each
4:30 – timed runs to 1b
4:40 – Monday Mile
```

Figure 1-6. Sample practice plan

A Typical Week In-Season

MONDAY:	Situation
	BP (batting practice) w/fungoes
	Conditioning: *Monday Mile*
TUESDAY:	Game
WEDNESDAY:	1-3 offenses and defenses
	Infield/Outfield/Pitchers/catchers: defensive group fundamentals and skill drills
	Structured BP: cone drill (drive the middle), RBI BP, collegiate BP, etc.
THURSDAY:	Game
FRIDAY:	Pick offs, Bunt and run offense, BP w/fungoes, Conditioning, variable but 1-3 sprints
	2B- home sprints are appropriate
SATURDAY:	Game or Off
SUNDAY:	Off

BP is never just a stand around. There are always stations to be worked through-diamond with live pitching, cage, tees, etc.

During Monday's "situation," be sure to build cutoffs, bunt coverages, 1-3 defenses, etc. into the drill. You need to prep them for the upcoming week and shake the weekend cobwebs off.

The Wednesday and Friday *Mental Practice* (i.e., pickoffs, 1-3's, bunt-runs, etc.) are interchangeable based upon immediate needs.

Building Team Concepts

Much of what has already been presented deals with building team concepts, but here are a few more considerations to keep in mind. First, help your team bond together, you may wish to schedule a team outing to a professional game or even an appropriate movie. A dinner out or even treating your team to an ice cream after a significant victory is helpful, too.

Never allow hazing. This is a barbaric and degrading ritual totally out of place in this time and age. You are probably aware of psychological studies that suggest that certain so-called *harmless rituals* like shaving the head, etc., tend to subordinate the individual to the team, and by breaking down individuality, make hazing a positive thing. Do not accept this supposed validation. In youth sports, not only can you get yourself into hot water professionally, but you can also end up losing kids. Even small things like having sixth graders or freshmen clean up the gear every day tends to break down team unity as it separates them. Rotate your clean-up chores according to grade or position, and even have a day when coaches and scorekeepers are responsible for postgame cleanup.

Make sure that every player on your team has a role. Certain players with minimal skills would be designated as pinch runners, middle-relief pitchers, pinch hitters, and so forth. Find a role for each child, even those that will never play in a game. They may be scorekeepers, B-Team baseline coaches, or even B-Team captains.

Rally cries are helpful, too. If it is a big moment in the game, call out, "Everybody up," which means that they are to hover by the fence or at the top of the dugout. As you complete your pre-game drills, have the kids line up along the baseline nearest the dugout. Make it a pep rally as they clap and chatter for the players finishing their pre-game infield sequence. (Do not do this when the outfield is throwing as injuries could occur.) Calling, "Team in," means that you are calling for a huddle. You should always bring them in before and after each game. During games, these huddles need to be used somewhat sparingly and always strategically placed. "Help each other in," can be called out during sprints and laps. This means that things are tough, the kids are dragging, and the players who finished first need to clap and urge on those players who are lagging behind.

If a player hits a homer or drives in a key run, everyone is to yell, cheer and show bench life. The bench empties to greet a homerun hitter as he crosses the plate. Similarly, if a ball has been hit and the player reaches base safely, but you are not sure if it was a hit or an error, call out to the bench, "Jury that one." Let the kids decide the scoring. You find out a lot about team attitudes as reflected by their generosity.

If your ball club wins a championship, arrange if at all possible for the local Fire Department to take the kids around town riding atop the fire trucks and screaming victorious shouts. This is fun for the coaches, too. The parents will love it, the kids will love it, and it can even turn a season-ending loss into a psychological win.

Again, if your team does wins a title, be sure to offer some sort of memento such as t-shirts, embroidered caps, or jackets. Offer them to the parents too, as they often lived or died during every pitch!

Avoid the personal use of last names. When addressing your players use their first names and demand this of all the players on the team. It may be appropriate to cite their last names in official capacities such as lists of players reporting when and where, but avoid this in personal contexts. A person's name is their identity, especially their first name. Barriers are created by the improper use of last names, and building team unity is all about breaking down barriers.

And finally, never let the players preen, gyrate, or showboat after a great play. Although this usually happens less in baseball than it does in other sports like football and basketball, you must still be on guard. After a great catch or a homerun, the player must turn immediately to his teammates, never to the crowd or the other team. Write this rule in stone.

Making Out the Lineup Card

Much has been said and written about the differences between the professional, college, and high school baseball game. But when you add in the middle school game, even more differences come to light. Whatever those differences may be, the following is a conceptual approach to making out a batting order:

1. The leadoff man must be a patient batter. He should lead the team in bases on balls and fewest strikeouts. He needs a good eye at the plate because a walk is as good as a hit in his case. He must also be fast and will probably be among the top base stealers on the squad. He needs to lead the team in runs scored.

2. This hitter must be a good contact hitter with the ability to go with the pitch and drive it to the opposite field. He must also be able to bunt and he should have reasonable speed.

3. This is the best hitter you have. Bat him in the three hole to maximize the number of times he will go to the plate. He has the ability to drive in runs with extra base hits, too.

4. This batter is similar to number three, but may be more of a long-ball hitter and may have a few more strikeouts, as he is a free swinger. His foot speed may be slightly slower, too.

4. This is third straight long-ball RBI threat you send to the plate, and this player has the ability to lead the team in not only runs batted in, but also in strikeouts. This may be your slowest player, too. Be aware that some kids have trouble dealing with the pressure of spots of one, three, and four in the order. There is less pressure in this position.

6. This batter is very similar to number two in the order as it is surprising how many times you will need a bunt from this batter.

7. & 8. These are your weakest batters who can still hit the fastball but struggle against the curve, or do not have confidence to hit higher in the order. Slower foot speed may be a factor, too.

9. Contrary to popular belief, this is not the worst hitter on the squad. You should tell your number 9 hitters that they are a second-leadoff man and the walk is as good as a hit. If he gets on base twice in a game, odds are that you will win. This spot is reserved for a slumping player or one who has trouble with the breaking ball, but nonetheless, has a good eye and has good speed.

Never wait to make your lineups while sitting on the bench before a game. The construction of the lineup is arguably one of the most critical items in pre-game preparation. Do it at home or in the office when there is a reflective silence around you. You should try to post the day's lineup on the baseball bulletin board on game day so the kids know they are playing and can be thinking about it during the school day.

And oh, yes—why not make up formal lineup cards with your school name and team logo and a spot for your signature? Type it all on a half sheet of paper and run off on colored paper. It is just another little thing that makes your team a bit more classy and professional.

By the Book

Besides the obvious differences—like salary and skill between coaching athletes at the youth level and coaching in the college and professional ranks—there are times when even *The Book*, or what is considered conservative and conventional baseball strategy, differs as well.

Here are some sacrosanct rules from *The Book*, and why youth baseball coaches are allowed to disregard some of them:

NEVER ALLOW THE THIRD OUT TO BE MADE AT THIRD BASE: With two strikes on the batter and a runner on second with two outs, you are sending him. Why? The catcher on this level may throw the ball into left field, hence the odds are better on the runner than on the hitter driving him with two outs and two strikes. It also may unnerve the pitcher and produce a walk that equates to a first-and-third situation or even puts the runner in a position to steal home on a passed ball. All things considered, it keeps the pressure on the defense.

GUARD THE LINES WITH A LEAD LATE IN THE GAME: No. You should play your corner infielders at normal width and depth. The thinking behind this rule is that the infielder guarding the line will take away a double that would put the runner in scoring position. On this level, a single often becomes a double when the batter-runner steals, as the steal is such a high-percentage play. Take away the infield out. Do not worry about the double.

INTENTIONALLY WALK THE GOOD HITTER WHEN FIRST BASE IS OPEN. Although there is merit in this thinking and you should never let the opponent's best hitter beat us, you should generally be opposed to the intentional walk. You can call out to your pitcher and catcher, "Nothing good." This means that first base is indeed open and a walk would not hurt you, so do not throw this hitter a strike. Work the corners or use the breaking ball. Why? Because hitters at this level are less disciplined and in an attempt to be a hero, they will swing at bad pitches trying to *hit one out*. They may fan or pop-up an outside pitch. You may steal a free out here. Also, as pro coaches will intentionally walk a hitter to load the bases, it is not recommended to do this even on the high school level. The home-to-first double play, which is the hoped-for result, is not a given on this level. Moreover, the unintentional walk that forces a run in often occurs because of the extra pressure on the pitcher.

RIGHTY/LEFTY MATCHUP, on the mound and at the plate? Forget about them on this level. Rely on better athletes with better skills to get the job done.

TAKING A STRIKE WITH A 3-0 OR 2-0 COUNT: On the high school varsity level , yes, but even on J.V., and certainly in youth ball, you should never use a take sign. You should teach aggressive hitting and give each kid who faces this count the green light, but with the cautionary words to look for his pitch. You could yell, "Zone it," from the coaching box. About the only time you want to allow a true *take* is from your hitters lower in the batting order against a pitcher who has had trouble finding the strike zone—or in a case when the pitcher has thrown two pitches and gotten two quick outs. You could call a time-out and tell the hitter to take the first strike in these instances, which are rare. When your are down a lot of runs late in a game, you will take the first strike, too, but you should tell this to your players in a huddle by the bench before the inning starts.

KNOCK DOWNS and BRUSH BACKS: The old axiom that the batter who comes to the plate after the guy who hits a homerun has to get knocked down, or that if one of your batters is hit, then one of theirs must go down, has no place in this level of ball. It is never justifiable. Even if the enemy pitchers sequentially hit your entire team, you would refuse to allow a retaliatory strike. Instead, you would complain to the umpires, withdraw your team from the field (yes, even at the risk of a forfeit), and fire off a brutal letter to the league commissioner, which would include, of course, a photocopy of the score book. You are dealing with kids here. Their potential lies in being injury-free, lessons in sportsmanship, and their future as players and as men.

There are some old baseball truisms that are appropriate to adhere to, even on this level of the game:

NEVER LET THEIR BIG HITTER BEAT YOU: Through scouting, reputation, or even after one time through the batting order, you will know who the big guns are. You should tell your pitchers to work very carefully with them, even walking them if need be. Often, these hitters will get frustrated when they do not see a good pitch to hit – and they won't – so they chase after bad pitches and you can steal a free out if you are lucky. The bottom line is that these players do not see any belt-high fastballs that they can turn on. They see a steady feed of breaking balls and pitches on the *black* (the corners of the plate).

YOU HAVE GOT TO GET TO GOOD PITCHERS EARLY: This is true quite often. Either through mindset, improper warm up, or whatever the case may be, good pitchers often find themselves in trouble in the early innings. So, if you are going to beat them, you must get to them at that point. Too often, the good pitchers get stronger as the game goes on. If your lineup is having trouble against a pitcher, you could resort to a bunting game. The hitters see the ball better, can put it in play more easily, and test the defense behind him. Plus, it can serve to rattle the good pitcher if you have placed runners on base or even scored a few cheap runs without hitting the ball out of the infield. Keep in mind that young pitchers may be significantly better from the windup than they are from the stretch, so this is another reason why you want to resort to a bunting attack.

CHAPTER 2

Practicing and Executing

The First Week of Practice

The opening week of preseason is the most critical time for your program. The players you've inherited have just come from Little League programs that may have been poorly run. It's now up to you to show them that they're in for something different—and special—because you and your staff are professionals—not dads—and they'll be playing for your school at a new level of baseball. Set a professional tone by posting your practice plans with titles such as *Opening Day* or *Day One*.

On opening day, teach players the proper stretching routine you intend to use for the duration of the season. Research has shown that light running should always precede stretching. Have them form pairs for buddy stretches. You should also include from the start an agility program consisting of quick-feet crossovers with an imaginary grounder fielded in the *alligator-chomp* technique, two-step crossovers to cover more ground, and track-back crossovers as players run down an imaginary, deeply hit fly ball.

Later in the season, once your catcher corps has been determined, add specific catcher agility drills (side laterals, quick-feet reaction drills, and knee drops, for example). You might also include a closed-foot batting stride and back-heel roll drill. Two sets of each drill take less than 90 seconds and can work wonders for your team. However, some coaches prefer to implement a form-running program rather than agility drills.

You could follow stretching and agility drills with throwing. You need to emphasize short distances (approximately 40 feet) and repetition, since the arm muscles must be trained for endurance like any other muscle group. Work on throwing at least 10 to 15 minutes each day during the first week. Although the teaching and training factors inherent in this daily stretching/throwing/agility practice plan may take up to 35 minutes on the first few days, it usually settles into a 15-minute routine at the beginning of each practice.

During week one of practice—fundamentals week—begin working through your checklist of skills that need to be taught during the season. For example:

Day 1: Hitting Fundamentals

There are two stages of hitting fundamentals: working the upper body and the lower body. You should first give a group instructional talk and a demonstration followed by approximately seven teaching stations, each no more than five minutes in duration. Use isolation drills for the upper body, such as batting tees, short toss, and so on. Be sure to impart the key words you'll use throughout the season to teach and correct. Don't use live pitching on the first day as nobody's arm—least of all yours—is ready for an hour of throwing batting practice. Day one concludes with the instruction of proper running techniques for beating out a ground ball, followed by a timed run to first base.

Day 2: Fielding Fundamentals

Teach proper form on ground balls and fly balls. Be careful not to allow too many long return throws. Again, use stations involving such things as shagging fly balls, wall drills, paddle gloves, and crossover drills. Form throwing and line drills are appropriate, too. Conclude with a mile run.

As you can see, you're teaching all the time. Even warm-up throwing has a teaching sequence with such drills as crow hop, snap throw, throwing from the knees, throwing with the feet planted, back-of-the-glove catching, and so on. (These simple yet critical drills are described in Chapter 8.)

Day 3: Live Pitching and Bunting Fundamentals

This will be the first day your players face live pitching. You should also teach and drill the fundamentals of bunting. Running drills include lead-and-steal sprints. You should use multi-station work in every phase of your teaching, that way some players hit live while others are in the cage. Others will also practice with bunt stations, pepper groups, tees, and short toss.

By the end of day three, you should also have addressed two areas of legal concern: sliding and catching fly balls in the sun. Too many court cases have arisen in these areas, so it's important as coaches to properly teach and drill these two techniques. See Chapter 5 for sliding tips and Chapter 7 for a drill that teaches players to safely catch balls in the sun.

Keep one group—middle infielders, first basemen, catchers, or outfielders—after practice each day for a 20-minute session to work on fundamentals specific to their position. Pitchers need more work, so bring them in on Saturday morning for a one-hour clinic. Invite parents so they can ask questions about the program afterwards.

The Daily Regimen

Every practice begins with drills for stretching, throwing, and agility, which take up to 15 minutes. As to whether preadolescents need to stretch, research suggests that athletes begin losing muscle elasticity as early as age 10. And no coach wants to lose a starting player for any game due to a muscle pull that could have been prevented.

Stretching

With the captains in the middle of the team circle, the stretching routine begins with toe-touches of two variations (Figures 2-1 and 2-2). Knees should not be bent and feet are together. Repeat this with the legs spread apart (Figure 2-3). From this spread position, stretch the groin area to each side (Figure 2-4). Keeping the legs apart, do trunk rotations, both twists and full clockwise turns of the upper body. The player is still standing at this point, and with feet together, he reaches overhead to twist an imaginary light bulb with fully extended arms and hands (Figure 2-5).

Figure 2-1. Standard toe touch

Figure 2-2. Crossed-leg toe touch

Figure 2-3

Figure 2-4. Groin stretch

Figure 2-5. Overhead stretch

Next, the player sits on the ground with the soles of his feet together, pushing the knees downward to further stretch the groin area (Figure 2-6). For the final stretch, he sits in a position resembling the numeral 4 illustrated in Figure 2-7; a bent leg slide is another way to describe it. He tries to touch his knee with his nose, then lies back, tucks the bent leg to the outside (resembling the hook slide), and touches the knee to the ground (Figure 2-8). Repeat this with the other leg. Some theorists suggest the hook-slide portion of this stretch may be injurious. Make sure your players do it properly, and do not overstretch. You may wish to add a supplemental quadriceps stretch illustrated in Figure 2-9, or the lower back stretches illustrated in Figures 2-10 and 2-11.

Figure 2-6

Figure 2-7

Figure 2-8

Figure 2-9

Figure 2-10   Figure 2-11

It is recommended to do this stretching routine before every practice and every game. It should also always be done after a half- or quarter-mile lap; the whistle blown to begin practice is the signal to begin the short warm-up jog. All stretching is done to a slow, methodical ten-count called out by the captains, without any bouncing movement. You should tell your players that they must try to increase their range of motion throughout the ten-count, with the muscle partially stretched at count number 3, more so at number 7, and fully stretched at 10. There is much research to suggest that 30 seconds is needed for a good stretch, but this ten-count will give you 15 to 20 seconds, which has been proven sufficient for this age.

Throwing

After the stretching routine, have your players pair off for the throwing routines described in Chapter 4.

Agility

After stretching and throwing, you should move to four vigorous agility drills. All of these agility drills are only done before practice, not before a game. The first two drills work on lateral movement and quickness. Players start in a good prepitch stance, with hands away from the body (not on the knees) and weight forward on the balls of the feet.

On a "Go!" command, they run first to one side and then to the other, using a single-step crossover. They should keep their shoulders square to the flight path of the imaginary ball.

Then work the same drill but with two steps to each side. Players are allowed to turn their shoulders, but when both steps are completed, they must be square to the ball's path.

Both of these quickness drills end with an *alligator chomp* as the bare hand covers the glove to catch an imaginary ball. The throwing hand moves from the top down to the glove in a kind of vertical clap, and then both hands draw the ball into the chest or abdominal area using *soft hands.* In this movement, as well as in the next one described, you're trying to build muscle memory, which kinesiologists tell us is so important for consistency in athletic performance.

The third agility drill covers all three body movements involved in hitting. Set players in a prepitch stance with the weight on the rear foot; the hands and back knee are in vertical alignment. Call out commands to "trigger," then "stride," and then, "swing." After the swing is completed, have players check their feet so see that the stride foot is closed, the front leg stiff, and the rear heel rolled.

The fourth and final agility drill is fly-ball tracking. Since fielders should never backpedal for a ball, you must break them of that habit. Facing a coach, they drop one foot back to the side the coach indicates by holding his fist overhead to replicate a fly ball. They backtrack using crossover steps, never taking their eyes off the ball (coach's fist). When the coach changes direction by swinging his hand to the other side, the players must react by planting, pivoting, and backtracking by crossing over to the other side. The drill is complete when the coach brings his fist down, as if the ball has died, and the players plant and charge back to their spot on line. Since each drill is done only twice, the entire sequence takes less time to execute than it took for the reader to read this paragraph.

Running Program

Upon completion of the stretching routine at each practice, use the following running program to enhance quickness, agility, and form. Each exercise is done twice and for a distance of about 20 yards:

- Short, choppy steps
- Heel kicking the buttocks
- High-leaping skips
- Backpedaling
- Side shuffles
- Carioca, samba-like moves
- Outfield-fade drill
- Lead and steal breaks

Indoor Practices

Rain doesn't mean your baseball practice has to be washed out. You can have a full-blown practice indoors.

Even if your squad is big, split them up so that half are being taught (say, in the hallway) while the other half is being drilled. Set up stations on instruction, hitting, pickoffs, first and third offenses and defenses, bunt techniques, and bunt-and-run offensive plays. Bring in pitchers and catchers for arm work or concentrate on selective pitches. You can work lead, read, and steal sprints indoors, too. Use your imagination and turn what could be considered a wasted day into a valuable one. Just remember that safety is a paramount concern in confined spaces, so you'll need to keep an especially close eye on the players.

Indoor hitting drills can include batting from tees against wall mats or a net slung over a door frame, hitting balls from the toss machine against the net, using a hand-held hitting stick, and so on. Use paddle gloves to work on ground balls and related footwork. Drop a base to work on double-play pivots with the middle infielders, or a set of bases to work on sliding—yes, sliding. Use old tarpaulins, rugs, or drop cloths. To work on pickoffs and first and third defenses, buy a set of rag balls or soft baseballs, such as those made by IncrediBall.

If you've been inside for an extended period of time, break things up by playing a game of distance or home-run derby—kids love it. Split the players into two teams and hit off the pitching machine. (You can use tennis balls).

You can also throw out balls so players can practice rounding ground balls and backtracking on fly balls. Work on charging grounders, catchers blocking dirt balls, pitchers covering first on balls hit to the right side, catching short hops, etc.

Want to send them home happy? When indoor practice is done, take them out in the rain for sliding practice! They love it, but warn parents beforehand that their child may be riding home soaking wet and muddy. Rainy days are opportunities to get a leg up on the opposition, because the other teams may not be practicing at all.

Creative Scrimmaging

After you have taught the fundamentals and instilled such basic skills as fly-ball drop zones, call systems, relays, cutoffs, and base-running rules, it's time for scrimmaging.

For your first scrimmage, play an intrasquad game. This will give coaches time to work on situations that may only arise in games, and allows you to work your pitchers and evaluate hitters. To help foster a friendly rivalry, have the losing team *buy* sodas for the entire squad. (You can buy a case of discount soda, and then each player gets one after the scrimmage—win or lose—but the losing players pay a dollar.)

Evaluation is essential to all of your scrimmages. The numbers go a long way in determining the ranking for each player. You should keep track of at bats, hits, walks, runs batted in, strikeouts, and fielding errors. At bats are counted in total, unlike the regular season when walks don't count against the batting average. Pitchers are charted, too; the pitch count is essential to prevent overworking your players.

The following are some drills to enhance situational opportunities and build a keener sense of game realities:

The 2-1 Count

Each hitter comes to the plate with two balls and one strike against him. This saves the pitchers' arms, speeds along the scrimmage, and helps prevent the hitters from looking for walks.

RBI Scrimmage

Start each inning with a runner on second. The batter knows that he must drive in the runner. This also works cutoffs and relays from a defensive standpoint. Check your runners to see if they're working their primary and secondary leads. Give signs to see if they know and can apply their running rules.

Set-Ups

Certain plays and situations occur infrequently during regular games, but you can set them up to give players plenty of opportunity to practice. By turning scrimmages into situational learning experiences, players will feel confident that they've *been there before* during regular season games.

For example, to practice a suicide or safety squeeze, begin each inning with a runner on third. Have the pitcher throw one strike. The runner steams down the line, the defense moves and rotates, and the hitter delivers the bunt. Upon completion of this do-or-die single-pitch scenario, take the runner off the bag, and the inning begins as if nothing ever happened. Or, practice a double-steal situation by setting up runners at first and third.

Don't be afraid to reset situations during the scrimmage (e.g., return runners to bases for another try if they've made a mistake) and never worry about looking bad in a scrimmage against one of your regular-season opponents. You want to see a lot of opposition runners on base so you can test fielders' arms and reactions. Also, the mental image of your team's abilities that your opponent carries home from a scrimmage can be helpful in the overall confidence factor during the regular season. The athlete at this age is especially judgmental, and this can work in your favor. (However, never let key conference opponents see your ace pitcher.)

Six Outs

Rather than changing the field every three outs as one would in a traditional game, clear the bases after three outs, keep the same team on defense, and go for another three outs before changing. This speeds things up considerably. Furthermore, there's a safety factor here as pitchers don't always allow their arms to cool off in chilly preseason weather.

Short Version of the Pregame Warm-Up

In high school and youth sports, not having sufficient time for a good pregame warm-up is usually the norm, but there is a way to maximize what little time is allotted. Tell the players to form a circle and have the captains stretch them and take care of pregame throwing while you exchange pleasantries and greetings with the opposing coach. Your starting pitcher should always have a game ball to throw with the starting catcher.

Once ready, all starting infielders, including the catcher, take their positions. All the other players report to centerfield for fungoes from either your assistant coach (preferably) or the designated hitter. The starting pitcher is warming up in the bullpen or on the sideline with the second- or third-string catcher. You and the catcher bring balls to use for the infield practice.

Use two balls at the same time for the infield drills. Don't allow players to chase overthrown balls. Have the catcher begin with a series of throws to each infielder stationed on the edge of the infield grass. Then the coach begins the fungoes with *one over, nice and easy* to first base. As soon as the throw is made from third to first, hit the second ball to the shortstop, then to second base. Two balls will be flying around the infield, so this must be practiced before actually doing it in a formal pregame.

The next infield throw is *one and around*, which means that the infielder gets a second ground ball, throws to first, and then the first baseman throws to second, second to third and third to home, as shown in Figure 2-12. Again, two balls are being used, so you must tell the infielders to stay back, refrain from charging, and hit the second ball as soon as the fielder releases the throw. Normal coverage, according to right- and left-side assignments, is to be followed at second. When you get to the first baseman's grounder, don't allow him to throw to second anymore as he has already done so three times; this throw goes to third base.

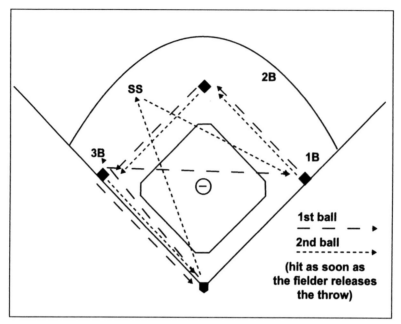

Figure 2-12. One-and-around pregame infield drill

Next, work a round of double plays. Create at least one instance where the second baseman must circle around to cover first, as well as a double play initiated by the catcher.

Include a *one and cover* in your initial series of fungoes if time permits. This refers to the infielder throwing across the diamond for an out at first, but then covering his base for a return throw from the catcher.

There are only two more infield throws to practice: the shortstop's toss to third and the bunt play with the first baseman flipping the ball to the second baseman covering. As you walk out to the pitcher's mound for the next round of fungoes involving both the outfielders and the infielders, roll a ball or two to the shortstop while the catcher rolls a ball or two to first.

Now it's time to bring the outfield into the scheme. With the cry of *starting outfield*, players know to jog to the bench as the starting outfielders sprint to their positions. Because mounds often differ in height, shape, and slope, have your starting pitcher take the mound to finish his warm-up. This is especially valuable at away fields. While the starting pitcher finishes his warm-ups with the starting catcher, you can use the reserve catcher for the next round of fungoes out by the pitcher's mound.

All outfielders throw to second initially. If time permits, they get both a fly ball to see the backdrop and a ground ball to get the feel of the grass height and field texture.

Then go to third with proper cutoffs. The pitcher by this time will have taken 6 to 10 warm-ups from the mound, which should be sufficient. You should then work cutoffs to the plate with fungoes hit from home. Be sure that the first baseman includes third, and even second, in his cutoff throws.

Close with the infield drawn in and the outfielders backing them up. Call the traditional *home and cover* or *home and in* depending upon time. In the home and cover, you fungo a grounder, the infielder throws home, and then he covers the bag for a final throw from the catcher. In the *home and in*, the infielder throws home and then charges home for a second ball rolled out by the catcher. End with a coach-thrown pop-up to the catcher. This short warm-up is so comprehensive—every throw players will need in the game is practiced—that you can also employ it as a practice drill.

It's important to build team unity by having the bench players line up along the third baseline to cheer as the infielders complete their throws home. This can even be a little intimidating to opponents as they get the message that you're serious competitors.

Bring the team in for a final pregame conference to review the signs and present a key message on the importance of the game. If it's a championship game, or you're playing a key opponent, the message is obvious—but if the opponent is weak, focus on one or two of the following themes: "This is a team you should beat, so go out there and take care of business," or, "I never care about how the other team plays; I want us to play like champions, so go out and do the job you're capable of."

Visual Signals and the Art of the Steal

The younger your players, the simpler your signs must be. Use alphabetical, object-related clues; for instance, since *belt* and *bunt* both begin with a *b*, touching your belt could be the signal to bunt. Likewise, *skin* could represent *steal*, *hat* for *hit and run*, and so on.

The signal should only be acted upon if you flash a *preassigned indicator*, such as touching the ear or shoulder, to designate that the signal immediately following the indicator is *live*—it should be acted upon. Without the indicator, no signal should ever be considered live, even if one has been flashed. If you think that the opposing team has stolen your signs, simply change the indicator and/or add a confirmation signal, such as a clap, when the sign sequence is completed.

Get in the habit of giving signs often, not just when a play is in progress, and get your team in the habit of checking signs regularly. During a rainy day practice indoors, it is wise to spend five minutes on reading signs.

If you see players looking for the sign, but you have nothing *to say*, simply point to them and call out something like, "Go get 'em," or, "Your way." But be sure to acknowledge that they have checked with you.

Many coaches ask for a confirmation sign from the batter or runner so that they know that the communication has been transmitted. A touch of the cap, or some other simple gesture will suffice. Some coaches even give players a request sign, such as tugging the belt and calling, "How many outs, Coach?" to request a steal. You reply with a shake of the head or the sign itself to accept or reject the request.

Professional teams change their entire sign series at different times during the season. But in 30 years of coaching, I've never changed mine except temporarily when my signs have been picked.

Pitchers and catchers need to communicate with signs, too. They need to know what pitch is coming and where it will be thrown. So a location sign must always follow a pitch sign, flashed by the catcher. The traditional approach is sound enough: one finger is a fastball, two fingers calls for a curve, and either three fingers or all waggling means a change-up. The location is signaled by a simple tuck of the fingers—palm up or palm out, for inside or outside to the hitter. A pitchout might be a balled fist and a pickoff might be a clenched fist followed by flashing all five fingers.

When a runner is leading off second, it can present a special problem for pitcher–catcher communication. If you feel the runner is looking at the catcher's signs and somehow telegraphing them to the hitter, simply change the sign sequence to the second sign. Many coaches use this formula: in odd numbered innings, the first sign is live; in even numbered innings, the second sign is live.

When your team is on offense, the same situation (a runner on second) presents an opportunity to find out where the catcher is asking the pitcher to throw the ball. If he gives the target signal inside, have your runner hold his hand out toward the batter's inside; hold it outside if the catcher is setting up there. To put it another way, if the hitter is right-handed and the catcher wants a fastball away, the runner leading off second extends his left hand back toward second while his right hand is tucked in closer to the body. This stance looks much like a normal leading position, so it's disguised fairly well.

To steal your opponent's batting signals, try the following method using two bench players: one stares at the opposing coach as he goes through his sign sequence while the other focuses on the hitter. Based on the premise that young, inexperienced players nod or turn away when they receive the live sign, your player looking at the opposition player should say, "Now!" when the batter looks away. The player looking at the coach remembers the last signal given. Have your *spies* compare what they perceive to be the signs against what actually happened before relaying them to you, however.

Look at body language. Many kids are simply not good at poker-face bluffing. Players in key situations may tense up or even grimace if called upon to produce in a big play situation; some even nod. Look at the opposition dugout. They may suddenly become unusually quiet and attentive when a big play has been called.

In other cases, a watchful coach can steal the catcher's signs to the pitcher by wandering out of the coaching box. He can look into the dugout and steal them from the opposition coach as he gives them to his catcher. Many pitchers tip their breaking pitches by over-rotating the ball in their glove after taking the sign from the catcher. Sometimes you can pick up a catcher's pitchout sign by watching his forearm muscles, which twitch when he wiggles his fingers. It's difficult for you as a coach to think about all this with everything else that demands your attention, but you can assign bench players to these tasks. It gives them a role, makes them feel they're contributing, and it may win a ball game for you.

CHAPTER 3

Hitters and Hitting

Teaching Hitting Part 1: From the Waist Down

Players must learn the proper mechanics of hitting to succeed at the plate. They may have been able to get away with flawed mechanics and uppercut home-run swings in short-fenced Little League parks, but such practices will return to haunt them in bigger ballparks against sophisticated pitching. It is vital to teach hitting from the ground up—literally.

Weight Distribution

The hitter should place about 70 percent of his body weight on his back foot. None of his weight should ride forward on the stride. Only when the bat head drives into the hitting zone should the weight transfer to the hips (never to the front foot).

Teach this by having your players trigger their weight back, stride with no weight coming forward, and then perform an *air swing*. They should feel the weight shifting to their hips and be balanced at the point of contact. Have them hop to test their balance. Test whether they're moving forward on the stride by placing your foot on the shadow cast on the ground by a batter's head—then as they stride, the shadow should remain under your foot.

The Feet

The hitter's feet should be shoulder width apart. Both toes should point to the opposite batter's box. If a hitter tends to fly open and pull off the ball, you can have him tuck his front toe inward.

Footwork: The Stride

As noted previously, the hitter shouldn't shift any weight forward on the stride; lunging makes him susceptible to off-speed pitches and breaking balls. The front foot must remain *closed* when striding. In other words, the hitter shouldn't open his front toe toward the pitcher when he strides. Keeping the stride toe pointed toward the opposite batter's box prevents *flying open* and pulling off the ball.

Realistically, the toe opens slightly. In fact, some hitting coaches call for a 45-degree opening of the front foot. But younger players have difficulty envisioning such a strict angle, so you should overemphasize it by insisting on a closed front toe. Also, a hitter should stride onto the ball of his front foot, never flat-footed, with the heel slightly off the ground on the stride (see Figure 3-1).

Figure 3-1. The heel of the stride foot should be off the ground slightly.

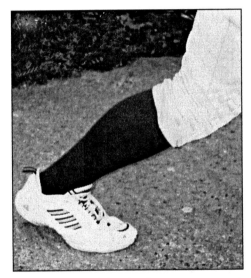

Figure 3-2. Back-heel roll

Footwork: The Back-Heel Roll

Envision the back foot connected to the inside hip. As the hips begin a rotation toward the ball, the hands bring the bat head down into the hitting zone. The back heel rolls upward simultaneously (see Figure 3-2). This entire movement should be coordinated and fluid with the heel, hip, and hands moving in unison. Many coaches use the phrase squash the bug or put out the cigarette to describe the action of the back heel.

The Trigger

There are two ways to set the weight on the back foot: first, shift the weight back from a balanced stance when the pitcher arrives at his release point (this is called the *trigger*); second, set the weight on the back foot *prior* to any movement by the pitcher (this is called the *preset trigger*—Major league hitters use both techniques). Either way is correct, so allow your players to use whichever is more comfortable for them.

The key point about the *trigger* is to make sure that the front arm position doesn't flatten out and the hands don't drop down. The hands and arms should remain static while the front shoulder turns inward and the back shoulder rises slightly. The hitter should also rise up slightly on his front toe. This movement is called the *trigger up*.

Teaching Hitting Part 2: The Upper Body

The Grip

Many young ball players have never been taught the fundamentals of gripping a bat, so be careful not to assume they know the proper techniques. It's common for inexperienced players to set the bat in the palms of their hands, resulting in a locked wrist when swinging. Instead, they should rest the bat handle across the calluses, just below the finger joints, as shown in Figure 3-6.

Be sure that the knuckles are aligned properly. When young players first grab a baseball bat, many naturally align the big knuckles with the middle knuckles, as illustrated in Figure 3-3. This is a power grip used to drive the ball deep. The grip in Figure 3-4 with the middle knuckles aligned seems to ensure better bat control, even though it may seem awkward at first. More big-league hitters utilize this grip than most people realize—it's one of the best-kept secrets in baseball.

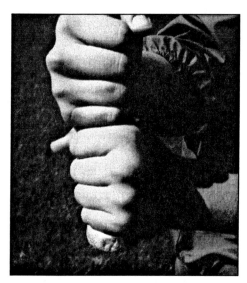

Figure 3-3

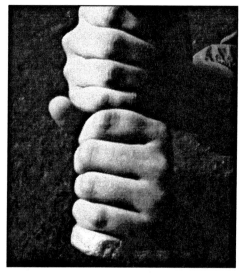

Figure 3-4

Explain to your players that the knuckle alignment can set up anywhere between the power grip and a linear alignment of the middle knuckles of both hands. In his book on hitting, Dusty Baker discusses a *modified grip*, illustrated in Figure 3-5, to place the ball in different areas of the ballpark. Figure 3-6 illustrates the proper and universal technique for gripping the bat.

Figure 3-5

Figure 3-6

Ty Hawkins, a hitting instructor in the New York Yankees minor league system, offers two important points about grip:

- Keep a tight grip with the lower hand and a looser grip with the top hand.
- With two strikes, choke up on the bat. Studies have shown that a batter can raise his average 100 points by doing this in two-strike situations.

Hands High

Hitters must set their hands high and at the top of the strike zone. For young hitters, this means at least atop their back shoulder (i.e., *up by their ears*). You should teach a line-drive swing with a downward approach of the bat that must begin with the hands held high.

The L Position

The front arm must resemble the letter *L*, as it does in Figures 3-7 through 3-9. This positioning enables the batter to bring the bat head into the hitting zone quicker. Too many hitters hitch by dropping their hands and/or straightening out the L of the front arm. Also, keep the front shoulder tight to the torso. Richard "Itch" Jones of the University of Illinois teaches this by having a hitter pretend he has a dollar bill clamped under his armpit.

Figure 3-7

Figure 3-8

Figure 3-9

Figures 3-10 and 3-11 show proper knuckle alignment and *L* position. The entire upper body torques up and back, while the hands and *L* position do not change. From this coiled position, the hitter tucks the front shoulder in toward the hitting zone and then drives into the pitch with controlled fury.

Figure 3-10

Figure 3-11

These mechanics are designed to help quicken the bat. This can be especially crucial for young players who may have been able to get away with a *drop-and-crank-it* style of hitting in Little League, but at a more advanced level they find that they can't catch up to a fastball, or, if they do hit it, they pop it up to the outfield. The sky-ball homer they used to hit in Little League simply gets caught by the shortstop or left fielder in this league.

Trigger Action

Use the fence rail as a guide in examining rotation. Although the hitter shown in Figure 3-10 could have his hands set back more, he's showing good triggering action. Note the inward rotation of the front shoulder and hips and how the hands trigger back and up without changing the L position of the front arm (Figure 3-11).

You should also check whether the front leg is stiffened when the hitter makes contact. If the player is bending his front knee, then he's lunging and transferring too much weight to the front leg rather than the hip. Hitters with this problem are liable to be victimized by off-speed pitches and breaking balls. Don't emphasize front-leg position; rather look for it as a cue that a correction needs to be made.

Likewise, don't emphasize raising the rear elbow because young hitters will think about it too much. Just see that it's on the same plane as the front elbow, or slightly above it, and make adjustments if necessary. If a young hitter is uppercutting, or if he's slicing his back shoulder downward, then see to it that the back elbow is raised. Otherwise, let it go as these two areas—the back elbow and the stiff front leg—can be over-coached.

The Downward Approach

Swinging the bat downward into the hitting zone is critical. Pro coaches like Jim Lefebvre call it the *power curve*, while others like Walt Hriniak saw it as *chopping at the ball*. Refer to Figure 3-12 for the proper downward-approach technique. Note how the barrel of the bat is always higher than the hands throughout the swing.

Figure 3-12. Downward approach

The key to it all is getting the bat head from the hands-high position down into the hitting area—and the route is crucial. It must make a diagonal cut across the torso. One of the best ways for coaches to see this is to focus on the knob rather than the bat head. It should drive across the upper body from shoulder to front hip, as shown in Figure 3-13. Then the bat head levels out as it drives through the hitting zone only to finish high. The route of the bat head, should resemble a *U.*

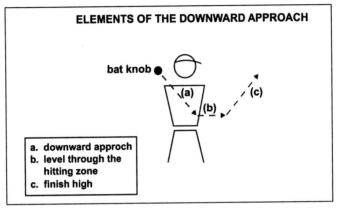

Figure 3-13. Route of the bat in the downward approach

Another point to consider as the bat head travels through the hitting zone is to drive the hands toward the pitcher rather than circling them across and outside the body. Keep everything moving on a line toward the pitcher. This style of hitting is designed to produce line drives and hard ground balls. The uppercut swings of professional hitters playing on fenced in fields is simply not what we mortals want to replicate. The statistics vary, but they say the same thing: more than 70 percent of line drives go for base hits, and 35 percent of grounders do, too. But less than 20 percent of fly balls drop in for hits. That's the difference between a .200 hitter and a .700 hitter. On your team, it's also the difference between a kid who plays and one who sits on the bench.

As for the follow-through, there's a huge controversy regarding the propriety of releasing the top hand off the bat, thus creating a *one-handed swing.* Some hitting coaches allow—even advocate—a one-handed swing, and conversely, there are other coaches who insist on the two-handed follow-through. It is important to note that the one-handed release comes only after the bat has cleared the front side of the body and the ball has long since jumped off the sweet spot. And for hitters who tend to pull their head out, the one-handed release can assist them in keeping their head in. Admittedly, big leaguers are not always the hitting technicians you want young hitters to emulate, but if you mentally chart the number of hitters now using the one-handed release, you'll find that it's a majority. An analogy could also be made with pitchers' deliveries. Years ago, a full windup over the head was considered sacrosanct while today the majority of pitchers use the no-windup delivery. And so the game evolves.

Much has been written about the art of hitting—there are entire books and videos devoted to the subject. But the checklist in Figure 3-14 will allow you to evaluate your hitters on their basic mechanics.

Hitter's Checklist

Stance
    ___proper shoulder width
    ___toes pointed at opposite batter's box
    ___feet parallel

Footwork
    ___back heel rolled
    ___front-foot strides with toe closed (45-degree angle at most)
    ___strides toward pitcher, not to outside
    ___back shoulder and back knee don't collapse (stay tall)
    ___trigger and stride separated

Weight
    ___triggered back

Shift
    ___weight transfers to hips
    ___trigger back and up
    ___L position retained during trigger
    ___hands kept high in trigger
    ___trigger preset with weight back
    ___hitting off stiff frontside (knee not broken)

Hips
    ___front hip kept closed (doesn't fly open)
    ___back hip driven to hitting zone
    ___balanced on follow-through (weight on hips)
    ___belly button to pitcher

Front arm
    ___shoulder clamped and closed
    ___in L position

Back Elbow
    ___relaxed

Hands
    ___proper knuckle alignment
    ___atop strike zone
    ___tight to body
    ___trigger up, not back
    ___bottom hand drives down into hitting zone (downward approach)
    ___top hand supinates

Arms
    ___extended

Head
    ___in and down
    ___nose to the bat head
    ___chin to the shoulder

Follow-through
    ___one-handed release
    ___follow through high
    ___shoulders level
    ___power curve

Figure 3-14. Hitter's checklist

The Principle of Going with the Pitch

When the ball is driven up the middle or pulled, the bat head leads ahead of the hands. When driving an outside pitch to the opposite field, wait on the pitch and lead with the hands. The route of the hand action is actually through the ball and out toward the opposite field. The hitter punches the ball right or left, depending on where the pitch is.

Leading with the Hands

When attempting to hit to the opposite field, three things are critical: closing the front shoulder on the trigger, waiting on the pitch, and *leading with the hands*. In Figure 3-15, the hitter is driving the ball up the middle, while in Figure 3-16 he's *leading with the hands* in front of the bat head and slapping the ball to the opposite field; some coaches refer to this as an *inside-out swing*.

Figure 3-15. Driving the ball up the middle

Figure 3-16. Slapping the ball to the opposite field

Teaching Hitting Part 3: The Mental Aspect

Players entering your level of baseball need to be taught plate discipline and control of the strike zone. All too often this isn't addressed in Little League. Not only will improved discipline at the plate make even your marginal hitters better, but also it will also greatly improve your team's chances for victory.

Ted Williams has a famous visual display at the Baseball Hall of Fame in Cooperstown, NY. He depicts a strike zone filled with baseballs, as illustrated in Figure 3-17. Each has a number on it indicating the hitter's hypothetical average if he swings at a pitch in the area where the ball is located. Obviously, hitting a pitch thrown right down the middle of the plate produces a higher batting average than one low and away.

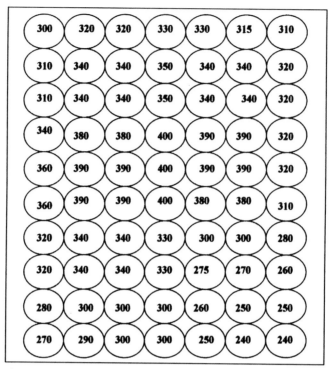

Figure 3-17. Ted Williams' strike zone and corresponding hypothetical averages for a lefty hitter

This leads to a set of rules you should try to instill in your players. Every strike has a rule.

The hitter should swing at the first strike only if it is *zoned* exactly where the hitter knows he can drive the pitch. For example, a belt-high fastball must be swung at and driven hard, but an off-speed pitch low and away, although usually called for a strike, cannot be hit with any consistent authority and therefore should not be swung at. You should insist that your players be selective and make pitchers throw to them instead of chasing a pitch. Eventually the pitcher is going to make a mistake and throw one right down the middle—be patient. The *first-strike rule*, means that the first strike must be your pitch. Otherwise, don't swing at it.

On the second strike, the hitter swings at any ball that is defined as a strike by the high school federation rule book.

On the third strike, the umpire's strike zone has to be considered. If the plate umpire has been consistently calling a particular area of the plate, such as the outside black portion, then players have to treat it as a strike and swing at it. It may indeed be a liberal interpretation of the zone, and in fact be a ball, but if the umpire has been calling it a strike all day, then it must also be a strike to the hitter. Don't protest, because for this particular game, that pitch is a strike and the plate must be protected there, too.

Since it's statistically true that most curveballs sail wide or below the strike zone, your rule should be to play the percentages by laying off this pitch. If the count or scouting report predicts that the pitcher will throw a curve, and if the hitter reads excessive spin on the ball, then he shouldn't swing at it. Instead, roll inward with a greater coil and *take one for the team* if the pitch doesn't break. Also by coiling inward, a hitter can drive a flat, breaking curve to the opposite field if he reads it and times it well.

Take a look at your statistics. Are your hitters getting enough base on balls? Is the walk-to-strikeout ratio greater than one-to-one? If the answer is no to either or both questions, then your hitters need to be more patient at the plate. Modifications need to be made for high school varsity where the pitchers throw more strikes, but certainly for youth baseball the one-to-one ratio can be used as a benchmark.

All this is not meant to imply that you teach your kids to look for walks—quite the contrary. It's not recommended to have a *take* sign for hitters at this age. You should stress aggressive hitting, but only on the belt-high fastball and on *your pitch*. With knowledge of the strike zone, a good eye, and plate discipline, your hitters—rather than enemy pitchers—can control the strike zone.

Hitting Flaws and Remedial Corrections

The following are some of the key mistakes that young hitters make, and some suggestions on how players can remedy them:

- Overstriding: Player will drop back shoulder and uppercut. Tie the shoelaces together.

Figure 3-18. Hitting flaw—lunging
(Notice "broken" front knee)

- Uppercutting: Shorten your stride. Raise your back elbow.

- Dropping your hands: Rest the bat head on your shoulder and drive into the hitting zone from there.

- Turning your head out (see Figure 3-19): Rest your chin on your front shoulder and see that it touches your back shoulder at the point of contact. (Teach the one-handed release.)

Figure 3-19. Hitting flaw—turning head out

Figure 3-20. Hitting flaw—flying open

- Flying open with the front hip and shoulder (see Figure 3-20): Turn your front toe slightly inward. Play short toss (described later in this chapter)and work on driving the ball to the opposite field. (Emphasize the trigger coil. Insist that the hitter's chest points directly at the pitcher on the follow-through to prevent over-swinging and over-rotation.)

- No weight transfer (see Figure 3-21) or too much weight shift (see Figure 3-18): Preset more weight on your back foot.

- Breaking the L: Work on your inward tuck (coil) with no upper-body hand movement. Work on triggering up, not back.

- Not rolling your back heel (see Figure 3-21): Run batless agility drills where you stride, and then with your hands up by your ear, slap a rag ball off a tee with the open palm of your top hand—your back heel rolls as your top hand descends from your ear.

Figure 3-21. Hitting flaws—no weight transfer and no back heel roll

- Poor or inconsistent contact: Play pepper with a half swing that stops at the point of contact. (Check with the school nurse to see if the player wears glasses in class and not on the field).

- Unable to hit off-speed and breaking balls: Practice short toss in the cage making sure you are hitting to the opposite side. (Instill the idea that a fouled-off curve is a victory because it was the pitcher's *out pitch*, and the player needs to come back with something else.)

- Improper hip action: Place the bat behind you with the middle of the bat in the small of your back and your arms crooked, holding the bat in place. Now explode your belly button toward the pitcher and emphasize your back-heel roll.

- Slicing the back shoulder under: Keep your shoulders on the same plane by holding your bat with two hands across the front of your shoulders in a cross-armed fashion—then swing. Emphasize your coil and keep your back elbow high.

- No separation: During live batting practice, have someone fake a pitch to you to see if you are striding properly. (Another check is to have the hitter trigger and hold the position. Place your fingertip against his front shoulder and ask him to stride. If any additional pressure is felt, then his weight came forward.)

The drop-step drill is good for correcting many flaws and teaching the trigger. Have the batter stand in a balanced stance with his weight evenly distributed. On the command, "drop," he should step directly back six inches with his front foot—don't allow him to open his frontside at all. The next command is, "Close up." He now steps back in toward the plate, and in one motion, swings and drives the ball off a hitting tee. Look for inward turn without dropping the hands with the weight going onto the back foot and then fluidly transferring to the hips. Also look for the back-heel roll and proper stride.

Still-Shot Photo Analysis

Developing mental imagery is as important as repetitive drilling to develop muscle memory, so you should photograph your hitters to analyze their swings. If you take the picture as the hitter makes contact, it's quite remarkable how much it reveals about head-and-foot position, arm extension, etc. Figure 3-22 shows several problems with the batter's technique. He is lunging, not finishing high, flying open (i.e., his front toe is open), and his front side is not stiff. However, he does display a good heel roll. In Figure 3-23, the batter has good footwork, weight transfer, and follow-through. He could, however, cut down on his stride.

Figure 3-22

Figure 3-23

Admittedly, still shots don't provide motion analysis, but if you don't want to lug around and set up videotape cameras and televisions, then still shots are a good alternative. Of course, if you can videotape, it's helpful, as is cutting out newspaper photos of pro players demonstrating good form—anything that can enhance the imaging process for your players.

After the photo analysis, give the snapshots to the kids—they love to see themselves in the photos anyway, and they usually end up at home on the refrigerator for the entire family to see!

Additional Thoughts on Working with Hitters

In the game of baseball, you must hit every day. If players need defensive work, schedule what is called *three-station hitting*. One station has defensive drills involving certain positions, such as outfielders, infielders, pitchers, and catchers. Another station may be bunting, and the third station could be hitting in the batting cage or on the main diamond. If it's raining, hit in the gym using some of the drills described previously in this chapter.

If you have a Monday game, you can offer optional batting practice on Sunday evening. Not everyone will show up, but at least you'll get a chance to work more closely with those who do.

Securing use of a pitching machine periodically is a good idea, particularly if it's the type that can throw curveballs. This is a great way to teach young players how to curl in and hit the curve ball to the opposite field. Pitching machines can be used either outdoors, or indoors with tennis balls.

As mentioned previously, don't use a *take* sign with your players—you want them to be aggressive hitters. Even if you're trailing by three or more runs late in a game, you should still go after every 3-0 pitch as long as it's one the hitter knows he can drive hard. You should be teaching your players to control the strike zone and look for the belt-high fastballs. Remember, this is middle school ball and you are prepping them for high school.

Kids have to be taught to hit the ball to the opposite field. Take an old home plate and draw lines on it with a felt tip marker, dividing it up into three zones as shown in Figure 3-24.

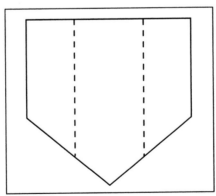

Figure 3-24

In the third of the plate that's nearest the batter, the hitter may pull the ball. Balls in the middle zone should be driven back up the middle, while pitches to the outside third must be driven to the opposite field. Remember, players must be taught to *go with the pitch* or *lead with the hands* and *wait on it*. These catch phrases are important. Coaching is the art of imparting mental cues that trigger mental responses necessary for the athlete's success.

A good drill to help you teach mental cues is called the *short toss*. Set a pitching screen 15 to 20 feet away from the hitter. Sitting behind the screen, throw balls like a dart over the outside edge of the plate. Using a short toss ensures better control of the pitch, and the hitter is less apt to free swing with you so close. The short-toss drill can also be used to teach players to wait on the curveball; they should roll inward with their front shoulder and hip, which has been termed coiling or triggering.

Wade Boggs' book, *The Techniques of Modern Hitting*, has an excellent section on recognizing pitches. He says that the curve always rises initially as it leaves the pitcher's hand and then loops down across the plate. This is his key to reading the curveball. Since most pitchers below the varsity level only have a one-plane or flat-breaking curve, the roll technique usually suffices. The two-plane curve (or "12-6" curves) requires more discipline and savvy.

You can even use the short-toss drill to teach players how to get hit with the pitch. You don't want hitters jumping back out of the box unless absolutely necessary, nor do you want them ducking as so many young hitters do. You should teach them the roll technique using rag balls. This drill need only be taught once in preseason, and it has the additional benefits of teaching safety, confidence, and hanging in there on the breaking pitch.

Another thing to emphasize with hitters is that their at-bat focus begins on deck. Teach them to think positively and to visualize hitting the ball. Each player on deck should imagine the crisp, frozen-rope line drive; envision the ball coming at him in slow motion; picture the perfect swing in his head; and look at the pitcher to observe his grip, his spin, and his release. Hitters should time their swings off the pitcher's speed and observe where the catcher is setting up behind the plate—inside or outside. Dry swings with weighted bats are an old on-deck standby. If the pitcher is slow, tell your players to use a heavier bat.

In short, on-deck time should be one of the most focused parts of a game. It's when each individual hitter prepares himself to do battle with the pitcher.

A Philosophy for Teaching Hitting

Hitting is perhaps the most over-coached aspect of the game. Many hitters have been ruined by poor advice. Remember the old adage, "If it ain't broke, don't fix it." If a kid is hitting .380 with slight mechanical imperfections, tell him about them, but don't harp or force him to change his entire stance or mechanics. No two hitters are exactly alike;

body mechanics are different for everyone. You cannot and should not try to make clones of your players.

Discriminate between primary and secondary flaws. Things such as hands held low, no stride, or not rolling the back heel are primary fundamentals that every hitter needs to do correctly. A slightly broken L position or hands not held quite as tight to the body as you might like are secondary considerations. By all means teach the ideal mechanics, but if a kid is successful his way, then don't force him to change; insist on change only when things are going badly and remediation is called for.

Creative Batting Practice

During batting practice in the old days, players stood around chatting in groups—usually about every subject other than baseball—totally bored while waiting for the pitcher and the batter to get it right. Modern batting practice should never be run this way. There are a variety of ways to focus your players and liven things up.

Bat Tree

A bat tree is an effective teaching tool, and a fun batting practice alternative. It's easy to make one yourself that is less expensive and more portable than metal and wood bat trees. To make the bat tree, drill five holes into a 5-foot length of PVC pipe and screw it into a base plate, as shown in Figure 3-25. Then, insert a 3-foot length of 1-inch foam pipe insulation into two or three of the holes, depending on the height of the player. Hitters will swing at the ends of the tubes, and learn to adjust for high and low pitches. Make sure to tape the ends and the middle of the tree's "arms" to minimize cutting and tearing.

Batting and Fungoes

Select your starting line-up on defense and hit fungoes to them in between pitches to the remaining batters. Infielders should throw to first. Outfielders are grouped in pairs to warm up.

Figure 3-25. Homemade bat tree

Collegiate Batting Practice

This is based on pregame batting practice in the major leagues and college ball. Divide your team into three or four groups of approximately four to five players. One group hits and chases foul balls while another shags the right side of the diamond, another on the left side, and the fourth works in the batting cage area.

The key is what the players do at the plate. A batter stands in and faces five pitches, hopefully all strikes, while another member of the group at home plate leads off first base. The batter drops a bunt to the right side on the first pitch as the runner breaks for second. Then the batter is asked to drive the ball hard to the right side, hitting behind the runner and moving him to third. The batter and runner then coordinate for a suicide squeeze. You should allow the batter to swing away for the final two pitches; he must run the last one out and become the new runner leading off first for the next hitter.

When all batters in the home plate group have hit and run, go to round two. Repeat with a runner on first, but execute the hit-and-run bringing the runner all the way around to third. The batter now has four pitches to get the runner in on a base hit or a sacrifice fly. Rotate the groups by moving them clockwise: right-side group to hitting, left-side group to the right side, hitters to the cage, and the cage group to the left side. The cage group is optional. You may prefer to use them as a baserunning group.

Cones

Have your players work on driving the ball up the middle by setting two traffic cones in the outfield in approximately left center and right center. Give them five swings to drive a base hit up the middle at least once. If they do this, give them three additional swings. If time permits, give them two more swings if one of the next three goes up the middle and one more if one of those two goes up the middle.

Two-Strike Hitting

This makes for a good finale to batting practice because it takes so little time. The batter stands in with two strikes on him. The pitcher is throwing batting practice pitches, but may throw breaking balls. Foul it off, hit it hard, and the batter stays up. Take a called third strike or swing and miss and he sits down. Allow a maximum of five hits and fouls. This moves fast, so keep a couple of hitters on deck and ready to go. Build a lot of chatter into the drills, too, as the players enjoy it—especially razzing each other if they don't hit the ball.

Bunt and Run

You can work on all of your reads and steals in this do-or-die drill. A batter is up and a runner is on first. The runner leads and steals while the batter bunts if it's a strike. The runner gets to second, and the batter then bunts him to third. The runner uses proper keys as described in the bunt–run game section of Chapter 5. Once the runner reaches third, he and the batter work a suicide squeeze, again with proper keys. The batter runs this one out and becomes the new runner. You can work this indoors and in several groups outdoors.

Working the Count

In regards to the mental aspect of hitting, it was stressed that you should approach every strike in a different way. It's a good idea to run your batting practice that way, too. Given six strikes, the first two are *zoned* according to the first-strike rule. The second strike must be hit where it is pitched, and the third strike must be at least fouled off in protecting the plate. You can do this with "short toss," as described earlier.

Pepper

Teach kids the time-honored *pepper drill*. It helps them learn to keep their heads down and in when batting. If you have a facility with limited space or even limited time before a game, you may want to break them into pepper groups. You can also use the term *bunt groups* for small groups of players—perhaps three to five of them—working on bunting form and placement.

Situational T-ball

Set a batting tee on home plate. Place your defense around the infield and outfield. Have the kids drive the ball hard someplace where the defense has to play it live. It is a simple drill that can enliven batting practice. It can also be humbling because it's difficult to really crush the ball as so many the hitters try to do. Work this same type of batting practice off the pitching machine, too.

Batting Cages

With indoor batting facilities currently in abundance, why not schedule a practice at your local batting cage? The kids will enjoy the change of pace, and if you work out a deal with the batting cage merchant, you might only have to pay no more than a few dollars per player. Indoor batting practice such as this is valuable during a chilly preseason or during periods of extended rain. However, remind your team to bring their own bats, because batting-cage bats are of notoriously poor quality. It might be wise to bring your team helmets, too, for safety and insurance reasons.

Plate Discipline

Emphasizing the *Count Rules* discussed previously (i.e.–*zoning the first strike as your pitch*—the second strike being the *book-strike zone*—and the third strike being the umpire's zone), throw batting practice with a specifically called ball/strike count. Again, the hitters must discipline themselves accordingly. This style of batting practice comes from Art Gordon, Head Baseball Coach at Manasquan High School in New Jersey. He does a great job teaching plate discipline through this method.

Battle the Ball Machine

Set your defense out in the field and have four to five hitters ready to go at home plate. Begin with the top of an imaginary inning. Players have to hit their way on base using good pitch selection, drawing walks (even machines aren't perfect), etc. The defensive team must shut down the offensive team while the latter must score. This involves cutoffs, bunt defenses, etc. You'll need to have a pitcher stand beside you to field bunts and cover first.

Bunting: The Next Level

The Pivot-Bunt Technique

When players leave Little League, you presume they know the double-hop-turn method of squaring to bunt. This is where the player's lead foot hops to the outside while the rear foot hops up to the inside simultaneously to square around and face the pitcher. To improve their bunting technique for high school and beyond, you should teach the pivot-bunt technique. The timing of the pivot is the same as the hop–turn: you start your move into the bunt position when the pitcher reaches the *hanger* position and his arm begins its delivery arc.

The actual technique, illustrated in Figure 3-26, is simple:

- The front foot steps out at a 45-degree angle—up and out about 4 inches—while the toe opens slightly. This provides balance.

- As the hitter steps out, the top hand slides up the bat 8 to 10 inches toward the middle, just below the *sweet spot* or bat barrel. The top hand employs the *pinch grip*—the fingers should never be wrapped around the bat head itself.

- As the bat is brought down to the bunt zone, the hitter rolls his back heel (pivots) just as he does when hitting normally.

- The hitter sights the pitcher over the top of the bat handle; he should keep the bat level or at an upward angle of roughly 45 degrees. He should never drop the bat barrel downward as a foul ball will almost inevitably result.

- The hitter adjusts to low pitches by dropping down at the hips and knees. He should never bend over, because that ruins the optical-sight line. Also, the hitter should keep the bat at the top of the strike zone so he has a reference point—and he should never chase a pitch above his hands unless it's a do-or-die situation.

- The hitter must extend his arms so that any bunt dropping straight down will land in fair territory. You probably shouldn't teach any *give* to the bat as the bunt is delivered. You may not agree with this, but keep in mind that it creates excessive movement on the bat head—the best bunts are delivered with perfectly still bats. If you're playing on artificial turf, then some give might be necessary. Remember, you have aluminum bats that are livelier than wooden ones. (When the pros teach bunting, they ask the hitter to *give* with the pitch, but that's with wooden bats.)

- To place the bunt or direct it down the baselines away from the pitcher, aim the bat label toward the shortstop or the second baseman to create the necessary angle.

Figure 3-26. Pivot bunt technique

Teach players that the more important the bunt—such as a sacrifice in a crucial situation or a suicide squeeze—the earlier the set–up must be. The pivot technique can also be used as a surprise play when the hitter wishes to bunt for a base hit. The hitter always has the option if nobody is on base; if someone is on, then the coach always signals bunts.

Another advantage this technique offers is that it's easier to fake the bunt and slash a base hit to the opposite field. The bunting hitter simply "shows bunt" (see Figure 3-27), then pulls back in with his front foot, tucks his front shoulder, and runs his lower hand up the bat to a good choke position, as shown in Figure 3-28. He must keep his hands high in the strike zone and get on top of the ball. The optimal base hit in this circumstance (for a right-handed batter) is a hard ground ball to the right side. With all the infielders moving to cover the supposed bunt, you can use this play to hit and run.

Two keys to effectively work this play from the batter's standpoint are:

- Close up the front side and tuck the front shoulder.
- Keep the hands high—resist the temptation to drop them—and get on top of the ball.

Figure 3-27. Hitter "shows bunt."

Figure 3-28. Batter moves back to hitting position from bunting stance.

CHAPTER 4

Pitching and Pitchers

Strengthening the Pitchers' Arms

Most adolescent pitchers need to be taught how to strengthen their arms and then care for them after they've pitched. The following exercises will help your pitchers accomplish this while preventing future injuries.

Football Throw

One strengthening technique, used by Tom House, pitching coach of the Texas Rangers, is to have pitchers throw a football with another player. This works to overload the arm and build muscle.

Tennis-Can Program

Another way to build strength involves tennis cans filled with sand (or cement), weighing about three pounds each. Tennis cans are inexpensive and approximately the same diameter as a baseball. Have your pitchers (catchers can benefit, too) do the following routine prior to each practice—it only takes a few minutes:

- Grab a filled tennis can with your pitching arm and bend at the waist. Let gravity do the work as your arm hangs limply. Slowly rotate the can clockwise in ever-larger circles; repeat counterclockwise. Perform 20 to 30 repetitions in each direction (Figure 4-1).

- Stand upright with the tennis can at arm's length down to your side. Raise your fully extended arm straight up over your head. Perform 15 to 20 repetitions (Figure 4-2).

Figure 4-1

- Hold the can behind your head. Straighten your arm from a bent-elbow position to straight out in front at eye level. Again, do 15 to 20 reps (Figure 4-3).

Figure 4-2

Figure 4-3

- Hold the can at your side and raise it in front of your body to eye level with your arm fully extended. Then rotate your thumb downward so your arm torques inward. This works the rotator cuff and should be performed in sets of 15 to 20 repetitions.

Instead of tennis cans, you can also use weighted or waterlogged baseballs, as long as they don't weigh more than 12 ounces each. Perform wrist rolls, supination, and pronation movements with the weighted balls. Add in some short-toss throwing.

Long Toss

Another option of strengthening the arm is the *long toss*. Players normally warm up at a distance of 40 to 60 feet apart. After their arms are sufficiently loosened, move them farther away so they're throwing about 120 feet apart for about five minutes of work. Do this twice a week in the late preseason and early regular season. Have catchers perform long toss *from their knees* at least once a week during the season. In addition to being a great arm-strengthener, it can only be done with proper upper-body rotation and follow-through form. A variation of this concept can be seen when pitchers begin their warm-up in the bull pen from behind the mound.

Two-Man Isometrics

Another great arm-strengthening exercise series comes from coach Paul McLaughlin, formerly of Brookdale Community College in Lincroft, New Jersey. The two exercises should be a part of your prepractice stretching—and all players do the exercises, not just your pitchers. These exercises can greatly reduce arm soreness in the preseason. Two players are involved: one to push and the other to provide resistance. Each isokinetic exercise is done to a ten count:

- One player lies on the ground with his throwing arm straight overhead. As he attempts to bring it straight down to his side, the other player holds the throwing hand and very slowly resists the forward movement of the thrower's arm as illustrated in Figure 4-4.

Figure 4-4

Figure 4-5

- Perform the same routine, but this time the thrower's elbow is level with the throwing shoulder and bent 90 degrees as illustrated in Figure 4-5.

Elastic Cord Drills

You may have one of the elastic cords with handles specifically designed for strength work, but even cords without handles can suffice. Drill #1 is for arm extension, as illustrated in Figure 4-6. Drill #2, shown in Figure 4-7, isolates the shoulder and elbow by keeping the upper arm locked at a 90-degree angle while moving the lower arm (forearm) forward.

Figure 4-6. Elastic Cord Drill #1

Figure 4-7. Elastic Cord Drill #2

Care of the Pitching Arm

Coaches must be careful not to burn out young pitchers, even if a championship game is at stake. You may be tempted to bring in a star pitcher with two days rest to close out the final inning, but could you honestly live with yourself if that promising athlete develops arm problems from your lack of care? You've probably heard horror stories about coaches who sent the same player out to the mound each and every game simply because *the pitcher is the pitcher.*

The best advice in caring for your pitchers' arms is to pay close attention to them. The following guidelines and considerations will help you care for your young athletes:

- The youth and high school pitcher should throw only one complete game per week—no more. This would be a 90- to 110-pitch outing in mid- or late season.

- The day after the pitcher works, he shouldn't throw at all, not even in practice. Assign him an underclassman *caddy* who throws the ball for him even when fielding grounders or fly balls. When the team is doing prepractice warm-ups, the pitcher should run instead.

- Ice the arm after each outing of more than 50 pitches. Keep ice packs in your first aid kit. Have the pitcher apply one to his elbow and another to the shoulder area for 10 to 15 minutes. He should ice it when he gets home, too. If the pitcher has no ice packs at home, a package of frozen vegetables works just fine.

- A good preseason formula for developing the arm is to have the pitcher throw 25 to 35 pitches in the first preseason scrimmage, which typically falls about 10 days into preseason. A week later he can work up to 50 pitches, but they shouldn't be thrown at more than 80 percent velocity, and no breaking balls should be thrown yet. He should work on location and form. A week before opening day, he can throw up to 70 pitches, but no more than 90 during his first game.

- If you can't hold scrimmages as often as you like, have your pitchers work imaginary innings with a catcher calling balls and strikes over a regulation plate in the bullpen. You can have them throw batting practice, too, but neither of these is as effective and realistic as live scrimmaging. Two weeks prior to the first scrimmage, the pitcher should throw some batting practice just to get used to the mound and the distance. Limit this to 20 pitches at 60 percent velocity.

- Keep a pitching chart and count all pitches. This is much more important than keeping track of innings pitched.

- A pitcher should never throw back-to-back games. But if the starter from the previous game threw less than 50 pitches, you may use him at first base or even right field where the throws may be minimal. Of course, the best-case scenario is to use him as a designated hitter.

Pitchers also have to be careful during warm-up. The late Billy Martin, when coaching in Oakland, used the following formula for his pitching staff: 10 pitches per inning are to be thrown. For a nine-inning game this translates to 90 pitches. If it seems a bit much, bear in mind that his pitching staff were mature, professional athletes. Translating this to your players might mean 70 total throws, including the initial *catch* warm-up and long tosses of up to 200 feet.

Younger pitchers typically throw a few warm-up tosses and then call out, "I'm ready!" You should respond with, "I want 40!" Tell them you want 40 throws and pitches from the stretch as well as the windup. Be sure that they've worked all their *stuff*. They must use a catcher and then later ask the catcher what was working and what was not. If possible, assign a coach to the bullpen. For high school pitchers, this same approach applies.

You've probably dealt with sixth graders who play on a 90-foot diamond, and who may also still be playing in the final years of their Little League careers on a 60-foot diamond. You've probably heard *knowledgeable* coaches advising their Little Leaguers that it can be bad for their arm if they play on fields of both sizes during the same year. Hogwash! There's no data to support this view. In fact, occasionally throwing from a 60-foot mound distance may even benefit Little League pitchers when they throw from 45 feet—that's what long toss is all about.

As for fielders, there's simply no evidence, derived from either formal study or my years of experience, that arms are injured by the distance differential. In fact, working on the bigger diamond probably strengthens the younger arms, and they love to return to the Little League field where their arms can gun the ball across the smaller diamond with newfound velocity and confidence.

Another primary concern is for your older, veteran pitchers who throw for you during the week and then find themselves under pressure from their Babe Ruth coaches to throw on the weekends, too. This can be a genuine problem, so you must stay informed as to where else your pitchers may be throwing. Again, keep the channels of communication open with their other coaches and lay down rules and pitch-count limitations in no uncertain terms.

Good Pitching Form and Mechanics

Taking the Sign: Eight Points to the Hitter

The eight points are both shoulders, both hips, both knees, and both toes (see Figure 4-8).

Figure 4-8. Taking the sign

No-Windup Delivery Sequence

Elbows are tight to the body; the glove is in the midline, and chest is high (see Figure 4-9).

Figure 4-9. No-windup delivery sequence

The Rocker Step

Take a short step with the glove-side foot back at a 45-degree angle, as shown in Figure 4-10. The purpose of this step is to help clear the pivot foot for positioning in front of the rubber. Too many pitchers exaggerate the rocker step sending their body weight back, away from the plate, which is counterproductive. Also, if the pitcher prefers a full windup, his hands raise as he takes the rocker step. His hands should not rotate back past the beanie of his cap, and he must maintain eye contact with his target through the A-frame created by his arms (see Figure 4-11).

Figure 4-10. The rocker step

Figure 4-11. The A-frame

The Tuck

Avoid leaning excessively and maintain balance. Keep the glove at the midline with eyes on the target. Raise the stride leg to a position where the thigh is parallel to the ground and the toe is relaxed. Also note how the pivot foot is positioned in front of the rubber in Figure 4-12. High-school pitchers know this, but kids coming out of Little League often don't. Don't have your pitcher show the hitter his number, as some coaches like to put it. This causes over-rotation. Have him show his hip pocket instead.

Break and Stride

It's imperative that the hands separate at the exact same time as the stride leg begins its movement toward home, otherwise a problem known as rushing develops, and the arm drags behind with no body assistance (see Figure 4-13).

Figure 4-12. The tuck

Figure 4-13. Break and stride

The Hanger Position

The shoulders are parallel, the back of the glove is thrown at the hitter, both elbows are bent rather than locked, the wrist is supple, and the back of the hand is pointed skyward (see Figure 4-14).

Figure 4-14. The hanger position

The Delivery

As the pitcher raises his throwing arm, he pulls his glove to his chest or hip, as shown in Figures 4-15 and 4-16. Also note that the elbow of his throwing arm is shoulder high. The pitcher should point his stride toe toward the plate. To teach this, draw a line in the dirt from the middle of the rubber to home plate. The stride foot should land flat, not on the heel. Some coaches might advocate a longer stride than shown in Figure 4-15, but a general rule to follow is four to five shoe lengths on the stride. Also note how the pitcher has opened his stride toe, pulled his glove in, and has his chest out over his stride in Figure 4-16. Remind your pitchers to push off the pivot foot!

Figure 4-15. The delivery

Figure 4-16. The delivery

The Follow-Through

In a proper follow-through, the release hand is outside and below the knee, as illustrated in Figure 4-17.

Figure 4-17. The follow-through

It was discussed previously about taking still photos of hitters to analyze their swings. You should do this for pitchers, too. During a preseason scrimmage, take a shot of them at the break-and-stride point as well as during follow-through—this is very helpful and revealing.

Pitching Strategies

Every pitcher must have a plan; every plan must have rules. Every pitcher needs to know what to throw, when to throw it, and where to throw it in order to get the batter out. That is the main objective: getting the batter out.

The most basic rule you should teach your pitchers is to pitch to the *L*. (Envision a backwards *L* for a right-handed batter.) They should work the ball low, down by the knees, and on the outside third of the plate.

The second basic rule is the *first-and-third pitch rule*. You want your first-and-third pitches to be strikes. The type of pitch matters little, but you want to stay ahead of the hitter in the count. You should caution your pitchers that if a batter is a first-pitch swinger—and a reasonably good one—you should try to get him to fish for a pitch just out of the strike zone on the first pitch, and follow-up with a second pitch that's a strike. You should chart all this action, too.

The third rule is that you should attack your opponent's batting order. You want to work location fastballs to the first and second hitters; off-speed and breaking balls only to the third, fourth, and fifth hitters; and then challenge the remainder of the order by mixing it up. Numbers eight and nine must be outs and should see mostly fastballs.

Of course, there are always exceptions and variations to these *rules*, but they do serve as a solid, general philosophy. You want to limit the number of curveballs thrown by your younger pitchers, so restrict them to only the third, fourth, and fifth hitters in the opponent's lineup. On your level, you probably never want to give hitters seven, eight, and nine a breaking ball. They're likely batting so low in the order because they have difficulty with normal fastballs, so there's no need to waste a curveball on them.

It's good standard practice to throw a curve or change-up to a hitter who has just crushed a long foul ball. Or, for a first-pitch swinger, you should start off with a curveball. In most cases, if you want a particular pitch, you should call for it with a verbal signal. If you call, "Nothing good," it means that you can afford to walk the hitter (he may be the top hitter or first base is open), so don't throw a hittable pitch.

The following pitching strategies will also help your players.

The 0-2 Pitch Rule

You shouldn't advocate the so-called *waste pitch*. Since many hitters on your level lack the proper plate discipline and may chase on marginal pitches, insist on a curve, a low-and-away pitch (maybe even just off the plate), or an up and in. The bottom line is that the 0-2 pitch must never be hittable.

In and Out

Jam the hitter with two inside strikes and then *bust* one on the outside corner.

Climb the Ladder

Even though this is more of a pro strategy, you can still teach it. Throw the first strike low at the knees (in or out to a righty, but never inside and low to a lefty). Throw the second strike inside but belt high, and the third strike up and in.

Downstairs

This is a rule that's *written in stone* rather than a flexible strategy. It means that it's imperative to keep the ball low and work the strike zone at knee level—every time. Tell pitchers to aim for the front knee of the batter.

Aim the Breaking Ball

Many pitchers just throw the curveball without a plan. As discussed previously, you should tell your pitchers to aim the breaking pitch down the middle and just below the right-handed hitter's belt for a *fishing* strike that the batter waves at as the ball breaks out of the zone—or, aim at the catcher's left shoulder on an inside setup to get the batter to bail out on a called strike.

Work the Change-Up

Teach the three-finger, over-the-top change-up because it's the easiest to throw at this level. Have your pitchers jam the ball deep in their hands. Don't teach the toe-drag as it can disrupt fundamental pitching mechanics. You can also show them the circle change, as it may be effective for them when they get to high school and their fingers have grown longer.

Other specific strategies include:

- Against a hitter with an overly closed stance, throw low and inside.
- Against a hitter with a *wrapped* bat, jam him inside.
- Against a hitter with a hitch, throw high fastballs.
- Against a hitter who steps in the bucket, pitch low and away.

- Against a hitter who crowds the plate, jam him inside.

- Against an open-stance hitter who stands away from the plate (and stays there), pitch on the outside third of the plate.

- Against a hitter who swings late, jam him inside and never throw him a change-up.

- Against a hitter who breaks his front knee and lunges, throw breaking balls and off-speed pitches.

- Against a hitter who pulls off the ball (flies open), work low and away.

- Against any hitter who swings at inside pitches effectively, throw at waist level and above, high and tight.

Pitching Charts

Pitching charts are overlooked in youth baseball. Many coaches simply don't understand their proper use. The fact is that pitching charts on the youth level are entirely different in purpose and function than from the professional level. The pros keep pitching charts to record hitters. In contrast, your records should be for the pitchers. A professional pitcher wants to know what pitch a hitter nailed for a homer, what the count was, and so forth, as well as what pitch they threw to get them out. Your charts should count pitches, spot location, and identify what type of pitch was thrown to what batter in the lineup.

For example, you should be concerned when the pitch count is up around 90. You will need to know if the pitcher is throwing down the middle too much or throwing curveballs to the number-nine hitter. Your charts will show this, and a meeting to review these charts with the pitcher should follow every game. You'll want to know if a pitcher is getting the first pitch over for a strike to most hitters, and the location on the 0-2 pitch that the hitter nailed for a line-drive single. Only your charts can tell you this.

Figure 4-18 is a sample pitching chart showing one inning of an imaginary game. Every pitch to a batter is numbered in sequence. If it's a fastball, you simply write the number, but if it's a curve, you should circle the number. For a change-up, you should draw a square around the number. Other special pitches can be identified by drawing a diamond or triangle around the number.

Each number is written in the box representing the strike zone as it is seen from the pitcher's viewpoint looking at the hitter. The recorder must also jot down whether the hitter was a righty or a lefty, his jersey number, and his number in the batting order. The result box shows what happened on the final pitch to that batter; simply draw a line from the final pitch to the result box with the appropriate K or 1B written in. Record foul balls as numbered pitches; no special notation is needed.

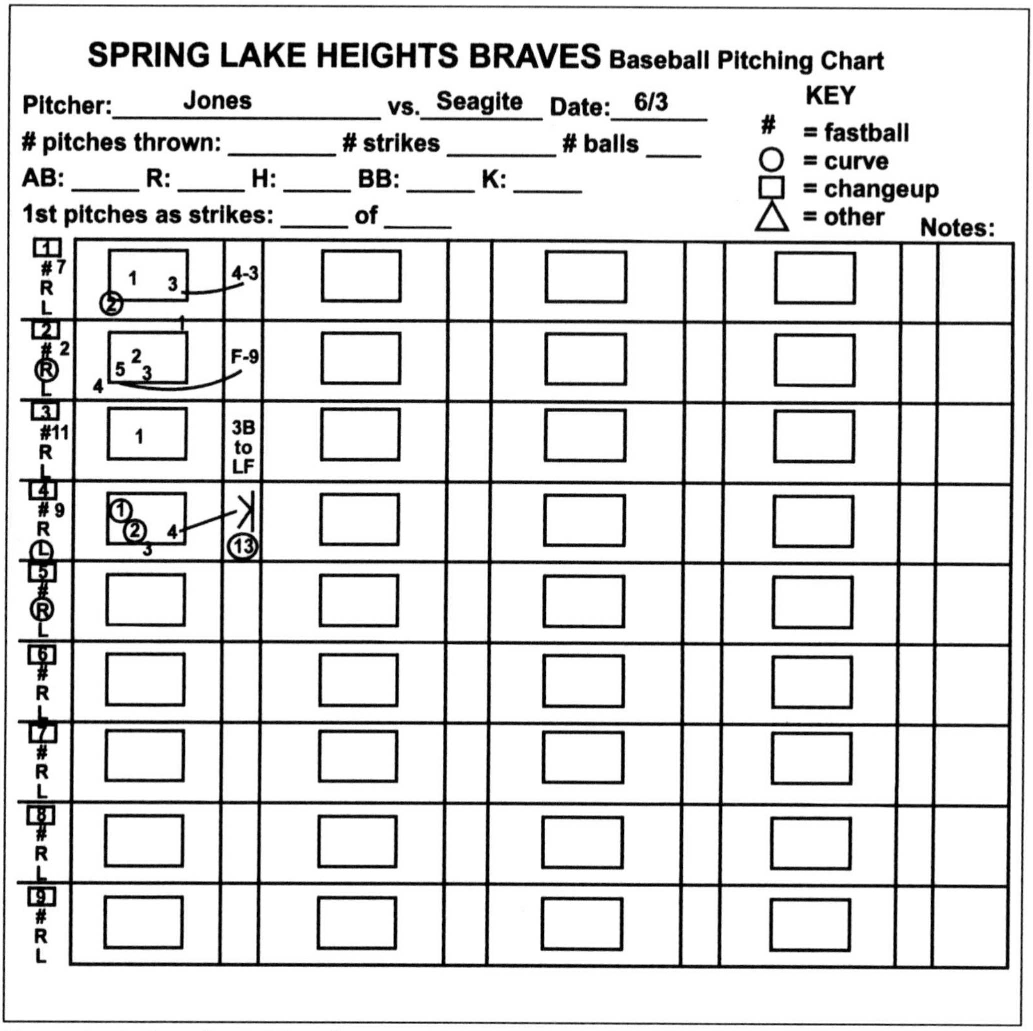

Figure 4-18. Sample pitching chart

At the end of each inning, have the recorder draw a dark line underneath the final hitter's box and total up the pitches thrown that inning. The next inning starts right below the final out of the previous inning. The pitch count is tabulated as a running total for the entire game.

You should demand that every player on the team know how to keep the pitching chart, but pitchers not in the game are usually directly responsible for keeping the charts.

Note the final tabulations at the top of each sheet. The section marked *notes* on the right side is for jotting down coaching points you spot during the game. For instance, you might call over to the chart recorder, "Elbow up on the curve," or, "Shorten stride"; these notations will then be reviewed in your postgame meetings.

Calling Pitches

One of the more controversial aspects of the modern game of baseball involves the question of whether or not coaches should call each and every pitch. Former Boston Red Sox pitching coach Joe Kerrigan says that he calls about 20 percent of all pitches while LSU's Stanley "Skip" Bertman openly states that he doesn't want to leave something as vital as pitch selection in the hands of a young catcher, so he calls all of them.

You shouldn't call every pitch, even on the youth level. Unless you have a pitching coach who can take over this duty, you simply have too many other things to worry about during a game. If you've schooled your pitcher and catcher on how you want to attack specific hitters and the lineup in general, and if you've imparted the strategy of pitching to the *L*, then there's really little need to call every pitch.

There will be times when you want to call a specific pitch, so here are some suggestions as to how to make those calls. If you opt to use these verbal signals, be sure to mix in false signals every now and again.

- The 22, 44, 66, or 88 call: Double-digits with even numbers means a curveball.

- The triple-digit call: Any three-digit number, e.g. 137, signals a pitch-out.

- *Nothing good*: As stated previously, you should be reluctant to intentionally walk hitters, but if first base is open and your opponent's *big gun* is at the plate, you may yell this out. It tells your pitcher and catcher that you want breaking balls and off-speed stuff on the outside corner of the plate. This call tells them that it's OK to walk this guy, but try to get him to chase a bad pitch in hopes that he pops up or grounds out.

- Location of the fastball: This requires a verbal and a visual sign. Get the catcher's attention and touch your shoulder, either right or left, to indicate inside or outside. Your left shoulder would be the same as the catcher's—inside to a right-handed hitter. It's a simple system that allows you to convey your intentions when a specific pitch is needed.

Some coaches will call out numbers suggesting the face of a clock (from the catcher's perspective looking out at the pitcher) to signal location. For example, a call of "9" would be an inside fastball to a right-handed batter.

If you do have the luxury of having a pitching coach, here's a simple set of signs you can use:

- Fastball: Touch the top third of your body—head and face area.
- Curveball: Touch the middle third—chest or torso and upper arm.
- Change-up: Touch the lower third—waist, hip, legs.
- Location: Use the shoulder tap in combination with the pitch indicator.

Traditionally, coaches will touch a sequence of locations on their head and face—nose, chin, nose, and ear. It is usually either the first or last area touched that is live.

It will surprise you how often you can steal the catcher's signs on this level of ball, even in high school. Catchers don't often hide their signals well. Also keep in mind that the coaching boxes are only lines of reference, not boundaries which must be adhered to, so feel free to roam a bit and see what you can pick up. If you do intercept the catcher's signals to the pitcher, and after testing their validity are able to somehow get word to your hitters about what pitch is coming, this can be an obvious advantage for you—especially against a pitcher with off-speed stuff or a breaking ball. You can use a simple call system to alert your hitters. "Hang in there," means that a curve is coming; "Go get it," or no call at all means a fastball has been signaled. Some hitters prefer not to know, so check with your players before employing a call system.

Pitch Grips

You should teach the four main grips shown in Figures 4-19 through 4-22: four-seam fastball, curveball, three-finger change-up, and OK change-up. In addition, have your pitchers experiment with various finger pressures (such as the middle digit on the curveball) or slight tilts of the delivery hand (such as angling the wrist to the outside on a four-seamer) to obtain different breaks. You should not teach the slider at this age because it may cause elbow stress. When teaching the curveball, tell players to use the "yo-yo" style, rather than the "turn-the-doorknob" technique. Again, this is designed to keep the stress off the young pitcher's elbow. These techniques and pitches can be learned later in their careers and with relative ease.

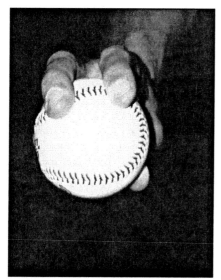

Figure 4-19. Four-seam fastball

Figure 4-20. Curveball

Figure 4-21. Three-finger change-up

Figure 4-22. OK change-up

Holding Runners on Base

The first rule of holding runners on base is the one usually forgotten: throw over to the base often. Keep the runners close to the base, even to the point of quick-pitching them (receiving the ball back from the first baseman and then quickly delivering it home before the runner can take his fullest extended lead). Let the umpire make the call if you are quick-pitching too blatantly. This coaching point is especially true off of second base. More often than not it results in a warning before a balk call, so learn your limitations.

Holding Runners on First Base for Right-Handed Pitchers

In coming to the *set position*, pitchers must remember two things: keep their hands high up on the chest rather than at the belt, and open their front shoulders to a point where they're perpendicular to the first base line. Both techniques quicken the pitcher's move and enable him to see the runner more easily.

Teach your pitchers a slide-step delivery to the plate with little or no lift of the stride leg in their delivery. Remember that pitchers must be able to throw strikes off this motion, so it cannot be too mechanically disruptive. Some coaches dislike the slide-step because it takes something off the fastball. You need to at least show your pitchers this move, bearing in mind their future careers.

Next, you should have your pitchers practice a sequence of moves to first base. Have the pitcher step off behind the rubber and throw over to first. He may prefer to do this twice in a row with the first step-off being a lazy *calling card* throw. He then repeats the move, but at top speed so that the runner thinks this is his good move. Either using one or two throw-overs with the step-off is the pitcher's only move and is thus easily read. The runner begins to curl his toes and itches to break. Now you have him!

Teach a balk move where the right-handed pitcher picks up his left heel (the front foot) presenting a steal-read because the right heel is still down on the dirt. When the front leg is only about an inch or two off the ground, he hop-spins and fires to first. Hopefully, the runner is leaning, but at the very least, you've confused him. Don't neglect to work on the strength of the throw-over. Moves are fine, but the quick arrival of the ball is crucial. Teach the balk move to your pitchers in slow motion at first and then speed it up so that it will be less detectable by the umpires.

Throws to Second Base for a Right-Handed Pitcher

Every pitcher should master two types of throws to second base. One is the simple yet quick hop-spin to second. This must be done *over the glove side*, which means the right-handed pitcher spins to his left. This provides a strong throw, but is less deceptive than the second technique. This is the move that Luis Tiant made famous. The pitcher lifts his leg as if he were coming to the tuck position (the thigh should be parallel to the ground) and then spins on his pivot foot (the one on the rubber), jabbing the lifted leg back toward second. This *Tiant move* is illustrated in Figure 4-23. You should try to incorporate this move into your pickoff plays at second so that it's done in conjunction with a middle infielder flashing to the bag.

Figure 4-23. The Tiant move

Balk Move to First Base for a Right-Handed Pitcher

In Figure 4-24, the pitcher has lifted his front foot off the ground and looks as if he's throwing home. In reality, he's coming over to first, as illustrated in Figure 4-25. When looking at the stop-action photos, it's clear the pitcher has balked, but when observing the pitcher in motion, it's very difficult for an umpire to perceive the balk. Teach this move slowly and robotically, then work on speeding it up.

Figure 4-24

Figure 4-25

Throws to Third Base for a Right-Handed Pitcher

It's imperative to throw to third if you suspect a squeeze play is coming. All pitchers are afraid to throw to third, so you need to teach this more and use it in the youth level so that pitchers can be confident and comfortable throwing over to third in the high school level. The balk move to first for left-handed pitchers, described in an upcoming section, can be mirrored for your right-handers throwing to third.

Check One, Two, or Three

This is a call from the dugout intended to communicate to your pitcher that the runner leading off the called base has an aggressive lead that he needs to check. He reins in the runner by stepping off the back of the rubber. Or he can throw a *calling card* toss.

Pitcher's Checklist

Prepitch
___ *Eight points to the plate* in taking signs

Rocker and Pivot
___ Elbow tight to the body
___ Short rocker step; 45-degree angle back
___ Glove and hands kept at midline of body
___ Hands don't pass hat button on windup
___ Shoulders in line with the plate, not *flying open*
___ No backward lean
___ Pivot foot steps in front of the rubber

Tuck Position
___ Stride leg lifted parallel to the ground
___ Eyes on target; head kept still
___ No over-rotation of torso
___ No excessive leg swing back
___ Balanced tuck position

Break and Stride
___ Break hands only when the stride begins—no rushing
___ Stride foot lands flat or on the balls of the feet
___ Stride foot lands with the toe pointing home
___ Stride foot lands in line with home plate
___ Back of the glove thrown at the hitter
___ Good hanger position with elbows flexed
___ Back of the throwing hand faces skyward; wrist is flexed

Pull and Deliver
___ Glove is pulled back into body on delivery
___ Proper arm arc, no short-armers
___ Chest out over stride leg (big chest)
___ Throwing arm elbow at shoulder height
___ Front leg braced on delivery

Follow-Through
___ Throwing hand is outside and below opposite knee
___ Recovers to field position
___ Trail leg follows after release
___ Toe of trail leg stabs the ground

Holding Runners

- Right-Handed Pitchers
  - ___ Open shoulder with runner on first base
  - ___ Good jump-turn move to first base
  - ___ Balk move to first base
  - ___ Knee-hang move to third base

- Left-Handed Pitchers
  - ___ Balk move (knee hang) to first base
  - ___ Varying-head read to first base
  - ___ No excessive leg lift or kick

- All Pitchers
  - ___ Slide step
  - ___ Spin move (Tiant move) to second base
  - ___ Throwing over enough
  - ___ Strength and accuracy when throwing over
  - ___ Step-off move to keep runners close

Pitch Grips
  - ___ Four-seam fastball, two-seam fastball
  - ___ Curve slider
  - ___ Three-finger-change, circle change

Miscellaneous
  - ___ *Stay-tall-and-fall* style
  - ___ Drop-and-drive style
  - ___ Changes arm angle for different deliveries

Aiming point on curveball
  - ___ Not tipping off pitch types
  - ___ Focus without emotion
  - ___ Good relationship with catcher
  - ___ Uses of batting practice fastball and heat
  - ___ Knows 0-2 pitch locations and types
  - ___ Backs up bunts; provides plate coverage
  - ___ Knows and uses pitching strategies
  - ___ Aiming point on pitch-out

If he chooses, he can work his pickoff move, but in any case, the pitcher needs to at least look at a runner when the runner has a big lead and you, as the coach, suspect the runner is breaking.

Balk Move to First for a Left-Handed Pitcher

This technique is illustrated in Figure 4-26. First, hang the leg. Second, allow the knee, with a sharp opening action, to present a movement home while keeping the foot in place. Use the fullest extent of the balk-line space when stepping toward first and making the throw. (The *balk line*, which is discussed in Chapter 5, runs perpendicular from the first base line to a midpoint on the pitcher's rubber.)

Figure 4-26. Left-handed pitcher's balk move to first

To make this move more difficult for the umpire to read, the pitcher should vary his head position, and if stepping slightly past the balk line, run off the mound as he throws. Teach this move slowly at first and then quicken it to make it more effective. Be sure that the pitcher can throw strikes off the leg-hang position.

Don't allow the pitcher to focus his eyes on the plate or first base. Rather, he should look at the dugout on the first base side and use peripheral vision to locate the runner as well as the hitter. This minimizes reading the head position as a steal key. His head should be locked onto the bench as the leg lifts to begin the pitch home or the throw-over.

CHAPTER 5

The Running Game

Coaching the Running Game

Winning on the youth level is in large part due to an effectively aggressive running attack. Even if your players aren't very skilled overall, you can still *steal wins* as you steal bases. You should set a *lofty* goal for stolen bases every season, keeping in mind the number of games you play.

You should always keep pressure on your opponent's defense with aggressive running, using the suicide squeeze, and taking the extra base whenever the opportunity presents itself. Young players at this level don't respond well to this kind of attack, making it possible for your team to *steal* the momentum from your opponent—no matter what the score.

First Base Leads, Reads, and Steals

Teach the *two-and-a-half shuffle lead* by having the player slide step to a lead of two-and-a-half wide steps. This places him exactly one diving body length away from the bag. He should never get picked off with this lead. Once the pitcher delivers to the plate, the runner is expected to increase to a *secondary lead* by taking two more steps, crossing over in a brisk walk, followed by a hop. This gets him 15 feet away from the bag and in good position to react to the ball as it crosses the plate. The same shuffle-step primary-lead technique, followed by the *one-two-hop* secondary lead, is taken off second and third base as well—but the distance varies, especially off second.

Every player on your team should have the green light to steal second base. If the score, or the strength of the catcher's arm prohibits this, then you'll have to adjust with a bunting game or abandon the steal altogether—but you should still enter the game with the *stealing* mind set. You may choose to give no steal sign; every runner could be expected to go within three pitches. They should vary their break and go on the first, second, or third pitch rather than the first one all the time. I call this the three-pitch rule in stealing bases.

Right-Handed Pitcher-Heel Reads

Reading the pitcher is critical. Against a right-hander, you should read his right heel. If the heel is down when the front leg picks up (as shown in Figure 5-1), then break with a hard crossover step toward second. If you see daylight between the heel and the ground (as shown in Figure 5-2), then this is the cue to hustle or dive back to first. You should reach across your body to enhance the upper body turn and grab the back edge of the bag with your right hand. These little techniques help avoid a sweep tag from the first baseman.

Figure 5-1. "Go" heel read

Figure 5-2. "Back" heel read

Left-Handed Pitcher Reads and Steals

Against a lefty, your first read is the right toe. When he picks up and delivers home, does the toe kick back across the front edge of the rubber? If so, according to the rules, he must throw a pitch. So, if the front toe breaks the plane, as shown in Figure 5-3, the runner should go. (Note: In NCAA rules, the back edge of the rubber is used as a reference.

If you don't have the toe read, then read the lefty's head. When he picks up his front foot, where is he looking? If he looks at the runner, as he is in Figure 5-4, he's going home; if he looks at the batter, he's throwing over to first base. This is true of about one-third of lefty pitchers on the middle school level.

Figure 5-3. "Go" toe read

Figure 5-4. "Go" head read

Failing these two reads, you're facing a lefty with an outstanding pickoff move and you must respect him. Be patient and read his front knee—the one opening toward home. Remember the balk line that runs perpendicular from the first base line to a midpoint on the pitcher's rubber, as shown in Figure 5-5. Once the lefty strides past this line, he must deliver home. The runner at first base must hold until the pitcher's front knee crosses that point.

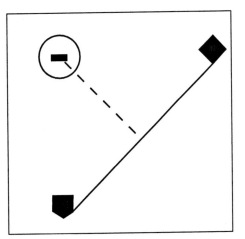

Figure 5-5. Balk line

Another key is the back shoulder. When it pulls away from the runner, go back as the pitcher is throwing over to first base. If it stays on line to the plate, then the runner should go. The problem is that this read causes a slightly late jump.

A very deceptive pickoff move for left-handers to watch for is when they open their knee while keeping their foot in a hanger position, and then jabbing the foot down right on the balk line. Very few lefties have this move at this level, but there might be a select few that can pull it off. Be aware of it.

On the youth level, perhaps 60 percent of left-handed pitchers will kick the front toe back, another 30 percent will give you the head read, and only 10 percent will have a really good move. In the case of a left-handed pitcher whose move is simply too good or too difficult to read, then you need to consider a *gamble steal*.

The pitcher's decision to throw over to first is not a reaction to the break by the runner; it's a response to the size of the lead off first. In the *gamble steal*, you should take your normal two-and-a-half steps and then break when the lefty picks up his front leg. You may get picked off, but since this steal is used only in conjunction with a sign, the coach calls it based upon the count or the number of times the left-handed pitcher has thrown over to first. For example, if the pitcher has thrown over to first twice in a row, he's probably not coming over a third time, so the runner should go. Or, if the count is 0-2, 1-2, or even 2-2, and you suspect an off-speed or breaking ball, then the runner should go. The three-pitch rule is off when the gamble steal is on. The coach will call for this steal, so no responsibility or blame is placed on the runner.

An effective gamble steal against a lefty with a good move will leave him wondering where and how he's tipping his move. A good quick break may even allow a picked-off runner to steal second ahead of the throw. A coaching point on running to second in this situation is to run at the fielder so that you're in line with his vision and the ball. This can be disruptive, and the throw may even hit the runner enabling him to arrive safely.

If you're coaching first base, remind each runner of not only the outs and situation, but also his reads and the three-pitch rule. If the pitcher has thrown over and the runner has returned standing up, then he needs to expand his lead by six inches or another short slide-step. Don't assume players will do this on their own; remind them to *work* their lead.

If you're facing a lefty, have the first runner to reach first base take a *one-way lead*. This is a normal two-and-a-half step lead, but with the pressure on the right foot ready to cross over and dive back in. The runner isn't stealing off this lead; he's trying to entice the left-handed pitcher into showing his move. Once you get it (and it generally takes only one or two pitches), then tell the runner to apply the three-pitch rule.

Modifications to strategy like the three-pitch rule certainly need to be adjusted in the high school level of baseball. You face better catchers than you would in youth baseball. However, even on the junior varsity, you could have a three-pitch rule. The techniques of leading, reading, and stealing cited here are virtually universal, but find out what works for your team. You should always be aggressive on the base paths at any level.

The Hit-and-Run

The hit-and-run is difficult to execute, but it certainly has its payoffs when accomplished. First of all, consider why you've called for this play. You may be calling it to keep pressure on the defense and force them to move around to open gaps for your hitters. If it's simply to advance the runner, there are easier and safer ways, since the hit-and-run can result in a double play with your runner caught off first base on a pop-up. You might utilize the hit-and-run primarily to cover your runner stealing second against a catcher with a great arm. You can also run it off a fake-bunt-and-hit (see Chapter 3). This forces the catcher to hold back a tad longer; it may result in blown coverage at second. Remember to show the bunt early, as this forces reactive movement and shifting on the part of the infielders. Also keep in mind that you should teach the pivot rather than the hop-turn square-around (Chapter 3). This helps in recovery to a hitting position. Once the pitcher's arm begins its delivery arc, have batters reverse their pivot, close up the front side, and slide the hands high. Ideally the batter will slash down on the ball to drive a sharp grounder to the right side, behind the breaking runner. Hopefully a hole has opened in the defensive coverage as the second baseman—reading either steal or bunt—has run over to cover first or second.

If the pitch is wild, have the batter lay off of it. You should have enough confidence in your running game to allow the runner to steal second on his own. It will be difficult for the catcher to throw him out when the pitch is an errant one, and you really don't want an over-zealous batter fouling the pitch off when you had the base stolen.

If the ball is hit, several factors come into play. Since the runner won't be able to see a hard grounder hit behind him, or may not be able to locate a pop-up, he must look for his third base coach who becomes his eyes. The coach will wave him on, perhaps even to third, or hold him up and send him back. Of course, if the ball is hit in front of the runner, he has some judgmental latitude.

This play must be practiced and its component parts isolated. Have your hitters work on fake-bunt/slash-hits during a special batting practice. Then add runners and a third-base coach to work their reads and keys.

Some youth coaches and commentators speak of the hit-and-run play succeeding with a left-handed hitter. It's fiction! Especially at this young age, it's difficult for a lefty hitter to consistently drive a ball into the left-center gap with enough authority to get the runner over to third. Remember, the ball is in front of him, and the throw is shorter, unless the ball is smoked between the outfielders. Instead, work a bunt-and-run with the lefty hitter. He can drag bunt if he likes, but you'd probably prefer a push bunt toward the third baseman. By forcing him to vacate the base to play the ball, your runner can make it if he has a good jump, rounds second hard, and anticipates the play. The ultimate goal in the hit-and-run or bunt-and-run is to get a runner on first over to third safely—two bases for the price of one.

Getting to First Base

Young runners need to be taught to *run through the bag* when they hit a ground ball hit, and to *round the bag* on a ball hit in the air. Rounding creates a better running angle to second and prevents a wide turn around first that would lengthen the route to second base. When the ball is hit on the ground, the hitter must assume that he'll be thrown out unless he can *beat it out.* He should drive hard for first with his eyes focused on the base, dipping his head on the final step before reaching the bag. This forces his body weight down and allows the lead foot to step on the near edge of the base a bit quicker. He then sprints past the base, but not too far, and never off the foul line. He should pull up before reaching the edge of the outfield grass, dropping his hips to facilitate this. He should also be looking over his right shoulder and locating either an overthrown ball or the coach giving further running directions.

As he sprints toward the bag, you should teach the runner to look at the feet of the first baseman. If the feet are coming off the base toward him, the runner must react by sliding to the foul-territory side because the first baseman is dealing with an errant throw and will attempt to tag him if he catches the ball. All this happens too quickly for a first base coach to command, so it must be an instinctive reaction on the runner's part.

As for a ball hit in the air—a line drive or a fly ball—the runner should assume it will fall in for a base hit, so he needs to be thinking about the possibility of advancing beyond first base. He needs to approach first by circling it or *rounding.* Sprinting down the line, he should veer out on the foul-territory grass about 12 to 15 feet from the bag, then cross the base by tagging it with his inside foot on the inner edge of the base to prevent himself from slipping. Next, he turns aggressively and looks for options as the ball is being played in front of him. The base coach will be of assistance at this point.

You should teach these simple concepts the first day of practice and only revisit them if corrections are needed. You could also work them into your conditioning program. You can drill these running techniques by lining the kids up at home plate and hitting ground or fly ball fungoes. Add in the first baseman's *feet read,* and your kids have a complete concept to practice.

Running Game Off Second Base

This calls for a three-step shuffle lead off second base if the runner is being held on, and a four-step lead if he's being ignored. The secondary lead is of paramount concern here. You want the runner to use his usual *one-two-hop* choreography, but he must arrive at a point one-third of the way down the baseline by the time the ball crosses the plate. From here you can steal, advance on a passed ball, or apply the running rules to a batted ball. If the runner gets the opportunity to sprint around third and race for home, (especially when he gets the *automatic* call discussed in an upcoming section) you have him take a step back toward the outfield to create a better rounding angle.

The runner attempts to steal third only if he gets a sign from the coach. If he feels he can make it, you should have a *request* signal; permission is granted depending upon the game situation, score, batting order, and whether or not the runner is getting a good secondary lead. There is no three-pitch rule off second because the runner is already in scoring position, so there's no need to risk him being thrown out on a steal attempt.

As for the passed ball, playing on a field with a deep backstop is nice because passed balls can occur as many as five times per game. You should teach your runners leading off second base that if they have a good secondary lead and see a pitched ball headed for the dirt low and outside, they are to break for third.

Runners with a secondary lead (one-third of the way down the line toward third) off second base are constantly reminded of the following *running rules*. These rules are simple, easily memorized, and effective in minimizing base-running errors:

- Ground ball at you or behind you: Go.

- Ground ball in front of you: Hold; retreat to second if the infielder checks you back.

- Fly ball at or behind you: Tag up. (College and high school varsity coaches need to modify this rule to read: Fly ball at you or in front of you—hold and read. As a basic rule, you should only tag on a fly ball behind you.)

- Fly ball in front of you: Hold and read.

Some clarifications are needed here. On a ground ball in front of the runner, the runner must hold to avoid being picked off—but on this level, a good play is to have the runner break for third after the throw, particularly if he hasn't been *checked back* to second base. As for tagging on a fly ball, you may want to shout out a signal like "Challenge them!" This tells the runner you want him to go if the ball is hit deep enough. You might make this call if the scouting report has told you that your opponent has weak or erratic arms in the outfield. Or perhaps this run is important and you need to gamble for a score. (Other verbal signals you can use are, "Be sure," and "Go hard." These are all described in a later section of this chapter.)

Running Game Off Third Base

The lead off third is the regular two-and-a-half steps, but with a step taken backwards into foul territory to prevent the runner from being called out if a batted ball hits him. You should emphasize a good secondary lead, which becomes especially important when reading the dirt ball or passed ball. Be aggressive on passed balls, but make sure to factor in such things as the game score, the number of outs, and who's batting in the lineup.

You should also consider the depth of the backstop. If the backstop is sufficiently deep to allow you to score, break for home the instant the ball hits the dirt outside the immediate home plate area. This is called a *reaction*. If the backstop is close, read the ball's rebound off of it and determine whether or not you can make it home safely. This is called a *read*.

There are three important rules you should have your players memorize and apply when running off third base:

- Ground ball: Apply the *automatic* and *normal* calls (covered under the section on verbal signals later in this chapter).

- Fly ball: Return to the bag for a possible tag up, even on foul pop-ups.

- Line drive: Sit and read. Go once the ball clears the infield on a base hit or error, but return to base if it's caught.

Be especially vigilant in teaching runners to sit and read on a line drive. Holding in their secondary lead position, they have enough time to either score or get back to the base. Young players will tend to react to a liner by hustling back, which can create problems. How many times have you seen this? The ball is nailed through the infield, but because the runner took a few steps back, he's thrown out at the plate. Delay meant his jump was late, which allowed the hard-charging outfielder to become a hero. You've lost both a run and an out.

Equally frustrating is the runner who tags up and leaves too early on what would have been an easy sacrifice fly. It's a good idea to implement these calls: "Bluff it," "Close," or "Safe." The first one is self-explanatory. The close call tells the runner he needs to hard key the catch and break the instant the ball touches leather. You can also use, "Challenge them," mentioned previously. If you call out, "Safe," it means the ball has been hit deep and the runner should score easily, so hold for a one-count after the catch is made.

It cannot be emphasized enough the necessity of specific running rules for this level of baseball. The running game is perhaps the biggest single difference between a 90-foot diamond and a Little League ballpark. Teach them the rules, drill them, and reinforce them on a regular basis.

The Bunt-Run Game

With bunting, stealing, and aggressive base-running, you can keep the pressure on the defense and the momentum on your side. Although you might have to resort to a bunting attack if your hitters cannot figure out a pitcher, this isn't what you want to accomplish with the bunt-run game. Effective bunting can also unnerve an emotional or physically weak pitcher, so that you as the coach can *play with his head*. The bunt-run game consists of simple rules for each base.

Bunt-Run Off First

If the runner steals, the batter bunts only if the pitch is a strike. It's preferred that bunter lay it down on the third-base side to put the third baseman in a coverage quandary. You hopefully have enough confidence in your running game that your runner will steal second.

The batter must pull the bat back if the ball is out of the strike zone. The exception is when you're running against a catcher with a great arm. Then you should call for the bunt to hold the catcher back and cover your runner.

Have the runner sneak a peak at third when he's near second on his steal. Many times the third baseman will have chased the bunt leaving third open. If the runner has good speed and a good break, he can continue around second to gain third. He should rely on his own instinct or the judgment of the third base coach.

Bunt-Run Off Second Base

Leading off second, the runner breaks *only* when the ball has been bunted downward. The batter is not in a must-bunt situation so he should bunt only at strikes. You could include a play where the batter shows bunt, and if the third baseman charges the runner steals third. This requires a prearranged signal based upon how the opposition plays you in this situation.

Bunt-Run Off Third Base

The suicide squeeze is indefensible if executed properly. You probably aren't as optimistic about the safety squeeze (the runner breaks only when the ball is bunted), but the suicide squeeze is a great play. This adds another dimension of pressure when you get a runner on third.

The keys for the runner on third during a bunt-run are as follows:

- When the pitcher begins his delivery home, turn and walk briskly toward the plate, which disguises the suicide squeeze until the final second so the pitcher can't make an adjustment. Gain ground here—don't be timid. The runner has to be mentally committed toward home at this point.

- Keying on the pitcher's stride foot, break for home when it strikes the ground. Good pitchers may adjust on a squeeze play and throw the ball at the batter or high in the strike zone. But if you wait until he lands on his stride to sprint towards home, it will be physically impossible for the pitcher to make any adjustments.

- This play is always close so the runner will have to slide, probably to the infield side of the plate.

- As for the batter, he *must* get a piece of the ball for the suicide squeeze to work. You'll need to practice at least fouling off errant pitches to protect the runner.

It's surprising how many times you'll see the ball skip past the catcher as the pressure of defending this play has gotten to the opposition. You can create even more pressure by faking a steal once or twice. Then, by having your live squeeze play set up by the walking lead, the suicide is even more of a surprise.

The Double Suicide Squeeze

Having runners on both second and third scoring on the same play definitely swings the momentum your way! Work the suicide as previously described, but have the runner leading off second run a straight steal off a larger-than-normal lead. If the defense plays the initial bunt by throwing to first, you may catch the first baseman napping by waving in the runner from second.

When you employ an aggressive running attack, there will be times when you guess wrong and *run yourself out of an inning.* Deal with it, because that's just part of the game. The positives of an aggressive attack far outweigh the occasional negative. Also, keep in mind that you may at times defy conventional *baseball wisdom.* If your team is good at a particular play, then it's a high-percentage one for you regardless of whether it is for another team. So don't just *go by the book*—play your own game.

First-and-Third Offense

Having runners on first base and third base results in something important—an out, a stolen base, a run scored—each and every time. A coach must have control of this situation. You won't win every time, but you must have a plan.

You should use two primary and two supplementary attack patterns. Each play is named after the primary steal key. Primary steals are off the pitcher and first baseman; secondary steals are off the catcher and a walk. (The defenses against all of these plays are discussed in Chapter 6.)

In teaching these, you'll sense immediate confusion if you're a first-year coach or taking over a program for the first time. Work them in scrimmages and situation practices as well as spending time in a teach- and-review session. They are good for indoor practices, too. After you've taught your double-steal offenses and defenses, review each of them once a week for 20 minutes—the time will be well spent.

Even on the youth level, you should demand that your players master the two primary steal plays off the pitcher and off the first baseman. A third play, off the catcher, then gets put in later in the season if you feel the kids are ready for something new. A fourth steal play, off a base on balls, is easy to teach and can be added at the coach's discretion. The final steal play to consider is the third-strike steal.

Key Off the First Baseman

With runners on first and third bases, have the runner on first take a four-step lead, daring the pitcher to pick him off. He should break for second as soon as the pitcher throws the ball (either to first base or home), resulting in either a steal of second base or a rundown. If a steal results because the pitcher has thrown home, then no further play ensues, but if the pitcher throws to first, causing a rundown, the runner on third may attempt to steal home. The key for the runner at third to go is when the first baseman releases the ball to second, taking care not be suckered by a fake throw. If done properly, this play should get both runners in safely. Don't allow any runner to break if the pitcher merely steps off the rubber—there's no key here. Just reset the play or call another. Teach this one first as it's the easier of the two primary steals. Also, be advised that it's particularly effective against left-handed pitchers.

Key Off the Pitcher

Ideally, you are trying to force a balk on this play. The rule for your runner on first is simple: break with no lead on the pitcher's first move after he touches the rubber. The first move could be a twitch, raising the hands—anything. Just go! The runner will probably wind up in a rundown between first and second bases.

The runner leading off third has no hard-and-fast rule; he must use his head and make a choice based on the situation:

- If the pitcher whirls and fires to second, he should go.

- If the pitcher runs at the runner going to second, he should match the pitcher step-for-step, and when the pitcher reaches the edge of the infield dirt or the runner off third reaches a point one-third of the way home, then he should go.

- If the pitcher is running at the hung-up runner near second and tosses the ball en route, then he should go.

- If the pitcher whirls and checks the runner at third before doing anything with the runner going to second, the runner off third holds and waits for the middle infielder to receive the throw. The runner off third breaks for home only when the second baseman or shortstop throws the ball to first. It's the job of the runner hung up between second and first to stay in the run-down as long as possible, especially with two outs. It's also his job to make the infielders throw the ball by sprinting hard between the throws and *not looking back*. If he glances back, the fielder is disinclined to throw. Your reads off third are predicated upon throws, not pump fakes, at this point in the play.

Key Off the Catcher

This offensive play mentioned previously, more commonly known as the delayed steal, should be used in midseason and only if the players have mastered the previous two plays. This play is particularly effective against a lazy catcher who's throwing the ball back to the pitcher erratically or less than enthusiastically. The runner on first base with a slight or even nonexistent lead breaks when the catcher releases his throw. A rundown should result. The runner off third uses the same keys as in the key-off-the-pitcher play. The opposition battery, rather than your offensive attack, creates the next two first-and-third plays.

Key Off the Walk

This play arises when there's a runner on third and the batter draws a walk. He jogs to first, gets a visual sign from the coach, and sprints to second without stopping. The keys for the runner on third are the same as the key-off-the-pitcher play, so mastery of that admittedly complex set of reads is critical. You may feel the need to signal your other coach when there's a runner on third and the count to the batter reaches three balls. Often times, it may only be a nod as you both sense what's coming.

The Third-Strike Steal

With a runner on third, if the catcher drops the third strike, the batter sprints to first. Send the runner on third home as soon as the catcher releases the ball to first. You will get something for nothing here.

The Catch-Up Game

Hopefully you won't have to tone down your attack and play a *catch-up* game very often. This means you're losing big—and it's getting late. If you are losing a game (for example, you're down by three runs with three innings to go), try applying the following rules to your game strategy:

- Take the first strike; not the first pitch, but the first strike, so a 2-0 count means that you take it. This puts the hitter deeper into the count, teaches patience at the plate, and drags out the inning a bit longer. Kids in desperate situations get overly anxious. This is designed to counter that.

- Advance on an error or passed ball only if you're 100 percent sure you can make it. There's no margin for error because you need base runners to score runs.

- The three-pitch steal rule is off. No one steals. Again, you need runners on base, and the gamble is too risky.

Using the Stopwatch

A stopwatch is generally of little use on the youth level (though essential in high school), but it can be a very helpful guide against a quick pitcher or a strong-armed catcher. The rules of using a stopwatch are as follows:

- The pitcher-to-catcher time, from initial movement to when the ball hits the leather, should be 1.5 seconds or less.

- The catcher's throw to second base should be around 2 seconds.

- Know your players' steal times from first to second. (Time them off their lead during preseason.) Then do the math to determine your call. For example, if the pitcher takes 1.6 seconds to the plate, the catcher is 1.8 to second base, for a total of 3.4 seconds, you're not going to send a player who runs a 3.6 from first to second base.

Fine-Tuning the Running Game with Verbal Signals

Besides the set of visual signals every coach uses for his team, you'll need to communicate to young base runners ideas, notions, and thoughts other than the basics. Imagine you have a runner on third, and you want him to break for the plate at the instant the batter drives a ground ball. In the pros they call this the contact play, and it allows you to score a run on an infield out. You should call out automatic or normal in this instance, and the runner will know exactly what you want.

Automatic and *Normal* Calls

On the *automatic* call, the runner on third breaks once he reads that the ball has been hit on a downward plane, also making sure that it's not a soft hit back to the pitcher.

On the *normal* call, the runner waits until the ball clears the infield. You should use this when you're on third with less than two outs, the heart of the batting order is coming up, or you're behind and need base runners late in the game.

Go Hard and *Be Sure* **Calls**

When you have a runner on second and want him to break on the batted ball with the intent to score, use the *go hard* call. It gives the runner the mental imperative that his run means something special, that he'd better round third base *hard*, and not throttle down to locate the ball. The only thing that would stop him would be the third base coach, who has repositioned himself halfway between home and third, flashing a *hold-up* sign.

The be *sure* call is more conservative. The runner slows up rounding third and locates the ball as well as the coach. In contrast to the *go hard* play in which the runner *must* obey the coach's sign, the runner can use his own judgment and run through a hold-up sign with the "be sure" call.

Look Two and *Take a Turn* **Calls**

When the batter drives a single through the infield, he will hear one of two calls from the first base coach. *Look two* tells the runner to be aggressive as he probably hit a double, but he can use his own judgment. He'll need to run hard, however, as it will probably be a close play. If the runner has a definite double, simply point and yell, "Go, go, go!"

If the runner hears *take a turn*, it means that he probably has only a single but needs to aggressively round toward the infield. The outfielder may muff the ball giving him a shot at second.

Be Aggressive **Call**

Use this call to tell your third base coach to take chances with the runner, perhaps have him break on a wild pitch, draw a throw with a big lead, or score from second on a base hit. If you say this to a runner on first, then you're telling him to steal second right away. To a runner on second, you're telling him to break quickly on a ball in the dirt. This call is often made with two outs and can override such reads as the backstop-dirt-ball play described earlier.

Lead to the Upfield Hip **Call**

The infield is drawn in and you have a runner on first or second. This call tells your runner to align according to the nearest fielder's upfield hip—the side of the fielder nearest to the advanced base—rather than by counting slide steps. From this position, the runner can easily make it back to the bag in the event of a pickoff throw from the pitcher or catcher. It also enables the runner to get a bigger lead, since he's not being held on. A runner leading off second, however, should not take a lead that's farther from the bag than the second baseman's position.

Down Call

Down commands the runner to slide. It's often accompanied by a visual signal. The first baseman *foot read*, employed by a runner who slides to avoid a tag, is an exception and must be a reaction on the runner's part.

Get More or *Plus One, Two,* or *Three* Calls

If your runner is leading off any base, you want him to extend his lead if he's not being seriously held on or even paid attention to. Or you may simply want to play with the pitcher's head. The call *get more* is a decoy call that means nothing, but it does distract the pitcher. When you yell out a specific number, such as *plus two*, you're telling the runner you want him to expand his lead by that number of steps.

This works especially well with trail runners. For example, your runner on third is taking his normal lead and the third baseman is holding him on. You want your runner off second to expand his lead in hopes of scoring on a base hit, advancing on a passed ball, or drawing a pickoff throw to enable the runner on third to break for home. Call out, "Plus one, plus two, more, more," until you're satisfied.

Sliding

You expect your base runners to slide on close plays, so you need to actually teach them how to do it. If you can't do it yourself, then enlist an assistant coach or veteran player to help you demonstrate the following four slides:

- Traditional bent-leg slide
- Evasive bent-leg slide
- Pop-up slide
- Head-first slide

It's not recommended to teach the take-out slide on the youth level. Let the high school coaches teach that one. On the youth level, double plays involving a pivot man who needs to be taken out are minimal. Plus, you would have trouble dealing with a scene in which one of your players took out a middle infielder, who then needed to be taken off the field with an injury. That said, consider that the bent-leg evasive slide is similar or even identical to what will be taught as a take-out slide later on, and point this out to the players.

You should teach all of these slides within the first three days of preseason practice. Tell your players ahead of time that they must wear sweat pants to practice that day.

Traditional Bent-leg Slide

Start by lining up the players facing you. Have them sit down on the ground and fold their legs into a *figure four*—the essential sliding position, illustrated in Figure 5-6. Next, have them raise their lead leg (the one pointed straight out) and bend the knee on that leg slightly. This technique helps prevent injuries that can occur if the athlete were to jam his leg and ankle into the base. It's also more natural than the traditional bent-leg with the toe outside.

Figure 5-6. Traditional bent-leg slide

Finally, have them lie back on the ground with their legs in a figure-four position. By lying down, they're making the tag target smaller so a sweep tag across the shoulders is more likely to miss. It also reduces the likelihood of getting hit by an errant throw.

Drill these techniques by setting up about half a dozen bases, and line up the players in front of them. Announce each slide and have them execute, one at a time.

Perhaps the most common mistake is the tendency to dip into a slide late. An effective teaching aid is to have the base runner slide under a rope held lightly across his path, about one-and-a-half body lengths in front of the base.

Evasive Bent-Leg Slide

Have a coach or player straddle each base and indicate with a slow, exaggerated sweep-tag motion, which side the ball is coming from. The runner must then evade the tag by sliding to the outside and grabbing the base as he goes by, or roll over to tag the base with his hand. While players won't often use the hand-tag in a game, the notion of evasive sliding is taught by exaggeration.

Pop-Up Slides

The pop-up slide must be used whenever a player's momentum needs to be halted going into a bag, or when he's fairly certain he'll be safe but anticipates an overthrow or needs to locate the ball. Sell this slide by telling the kids that it *looks cool*.

Demonstrate to your players that on virtually all bent-leg slides the portions of the pants that get dirty should be the foreleg of the leg tucked under and the buttock on that same side. The runner should push off for this slide. The rear hand can also be used to push off the ground, but may not be necessary.

The Head-First Slide

This is the most controversial slide in baseball—but it embodies hustle, desire, and an all-out style of play that coaches want their teams to exemplify. Coaches may offer statistics suggesting that a player reaches base quicker when he goes in feet first, but as a player drives toward a base, it's logical that by diving he gets there earlier. To reverse body momentum and slip the feet in first defies the laws of motion. Whatever slide you choose to teach your players, it is indisputable that the headfirst slide helps set a tempo of aggressiveness and hard-nose baseball.

Safety Tips for the Head-First Slide

It is important that players slide with their hands bunched into a fist to avoid injury to their fingers. They should always keep their heads down initially to avoid injury to the face, and then pick it up to locate the ball and the coach for further instructions. If a runner must slide head-first into home—and many coaches frown on this because of the danger of diving into a wall of catcher's gear—they should always slide around home to the inside or outside of the plate to avoid colliding with the catcher. Little Leaguers shouldn't use the headfirst slide; it's for more competitive levels of baseball.

CHAPTER 6

Depths, Cutoffs, and Pickoffs

Infield Depths

When coaching on this level, you should teach your infield players to position themselves at one of four different depths (shown in Figure 6-1), depending on the situation. In addition, you may want to make some slight adjustments depending upon the hitting tendencies of your opponents (as revealed in scouting reports or score books.)

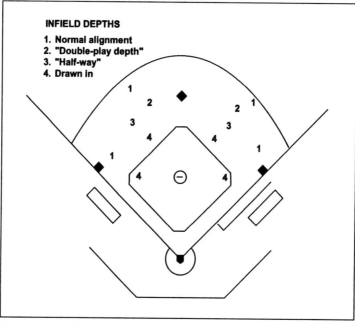

Figure 6-1. Infield depths

Normal Alignment

Most teams use the normal alignment ("1" in Figure 6-1), but remember one thing: statistically speaking, more base hits go up the middle. You should *bunch the middle* with your shortstop and second baseman.

Double-Play Depth

Move your middle infielders closer to second by having them take two steps forward and two steps to the bag. This alignment helps cover runners leading off second base, too.

Drawn In

All four infielders make this adjustment. The corners go to the edge of the cut in the infield grass while the middle infielders stand directly on the baseline. This inhibits the leading distance for a runner on second.

Halfway

If a runner is leading off third and you don't want to give up too much open ground—but still give yourself the opportunity to hold that runner on a ground ball—move the middle infielders halfway in. This sets the shortstop and second baseman exactly in between the drawn in position and normal depth. Another subtle component of this alignment is that it creates an element of doubt in the mind of the third base coach. If a hard ground ball is hit at one of those infielders, he questions whether or not to send the runner. And he who hesitates is *out*.

Depth combinations can be called out like, "Corners in; half-way up the middle," or, "Left side in; right side normal."

Drill the infielders' knowledge of these depths by sending them to the infield, calling out different alignments, and rotating wave after wave of infield contingents.

Outfield Depths

Figure 6-2 shows the positioning for each of the three outfield depths described in this section.

Normal Depth

Play the center fielder a bit more shallow than his counterparts in right and left. He generally has more speed and can run down balls in the gap or the flare zones more efficiently from a drawn-in position behind the shortstop and second baseman.

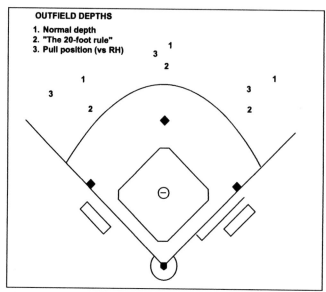

Figure 6-2. Outfield depths

The 20-Foot Rule

In youth baseball, you'll encounter wide discrepancies in the physical size of players. You can play the lanky eighth grader as if he were any high school senior or junior, but what of the diminutive sixth grader who just can't power the ball into an outfield gap yet? Play him with all three outfielders only 20 feet off the infield grass. Allow your center fielder to call this alignment; it keeps him thinking and gives him more responsibility.

Pull Alignment

Figure 6-2 illustrates the pull alignment for a right-handed hitter. Simply mirror it for a lefty. Be sure to draw in the opposite fielder, the right fielder in this case, since few hitters on this level can power the ball to the opposite field.

Special Plays

Special plays you can look for in youth baseball, but not necessarily in higher levels, are:

•. Having the right fielder throw the runner out at first on a line-shot base hit to the right. It happens more often than you think.

• Allowing your outfielders to throw through the cutoff man, directly to the base, from the 20-foot alignment. They're usually within arm range anyway.

• Having your center fielder throw to second for a force out of a runner on first on a hard hit ball up the middle. This presents itself especially for outfielders drawn in for the 20-foot rule.

Special Situation Depths

- Special Situation #1: It's late in a game and you're protecting a one- or two-run lead. Have the outfielders play a few steps deeper so they can keep everything in front of them. They'll be better able to run down *gappers*, too.

- Special Situation #2: You're the visiting team, and the game is tied in the bottom of the last inning. Obviously, a sacrifice fly ends the game, so bring the outfield in to a depth where they're certain to have sufficient arm strength to throw the runner out at the plate. But what if the ball is hit over their heads? The runner tags up and scores anyway. You need to take away the bloop single and line-drive hit to give your kids a chance to throw the runner out. This is another instance where you could call the 20-foot rule.

Fly Ball Drop Zones and Call System

Two fielders colliding as they both chase down a fly ball can be catastrophic. The ball dropping in between them as they both shy off of it can be devastating, too. You should teach the drop-zone responsibilities shown in Figure 6-3 and drill them in preseason with repeated fly ball fungoes. You should use the following rules in your call system:

- A fielder coming in for a ball can always call off any fielder who is chasing out to get it.

- In the case of two players calling for a ball, one must step up and make his call repeatedly. The other player should back off once he hears the repeated calls.

- If the issue is still not settled, the center fielder, shortstop, or catcher makes the call to settle it.

You want every fly ball caught during the entire season!

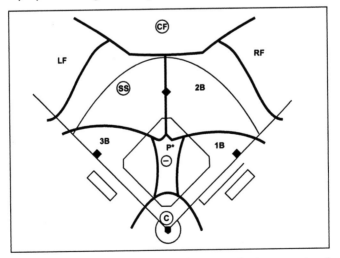

Figure 6-3. Drop zone responsibilities. CF is the *captain of the outfield* while the SS is the *captain of the infield*.

A Simplified Cutoff and Relay System

Coming out of Little League, the only thing the players know about cutoffs is to get the ball to the pitcher. A simple system like this leaves you with inadequate backup, poor overall positioning, and idle players who could be better utilized. It's important that they learn a system they'll encounter later on in high school. Don't hesitate to contact the local high school coach to inquire what cutoff and relay system he prefers. Then implement it if it's a system that works for you and your team.

First of all, you need to distinguish between a cutoff system and a relay system. In a cutoff system the play is *clean*, meaning the outfielder has come up with the ball directly and has to throw a runner out at the plate. In a relay system, the ball has gotten past the outfielders.

The Cutoff System

In a cutoff play, you should use the corner infielders as the cutoff men. Draw an imaginary line from home plate through the shortstop into left field. Any ball hit to the right of that line will be handled by the first baseman, who must recognize it and hustle into position. Any ball hit to the left of that imaginary line belongs to the third baseman. The reason for the differentiation is that on a ball sharply hit to the left, it's very difficult for the first baseman to arrive in time for an effective cutoff play, so have the third baseman take it with the shortstop rotating to cover third base.

Teach both cutoff men the concept known as *the box*: an imaginary square running from the pitcher's rubber to right angles on the baselines. The cutoff man should never be inside this box. Similarly, he should rarely be on the infield dirt.

The cutoff men should know the strength of the outfielders' arms and adjust by moving in or out for the ball. Cutoff men also need to be taught to move out to catch an under thrown ball that must be caught in flight. A thrown ball has a unique spin so will often take a weird bounce, thus negating an effective cutoff or relay. Insist on *leather-to-leather* execution in your drills. Any missed or muffed throws kill the play.

Emphasize proper signals and specifically raised arms, as well as proper mechanics such as turning the body to catch the ball. The receiver should turn his body with his glove side toward his target, then catch the ball across his body, step, and fire. Insist players use two hands and throw to the face and chest. Also, contrary to Little League ball, you want the pitcher out of the way. His sole responsibility is to provide backup by running to the foul territory off the third base line to back up either home or third as he reads the play. If the ball skips into dead ball territory, he's to blame.

Proper calls must be made, too. Besides signaling the cutoff man to align with calls such as "right, right, right" or "left, left, left," he must know that cut means to catch the ball—while no call means to let it go through. The follow-up commands are very important:

- *Cut one* means catch and throw to first (rarely used).
- *Cut two* means catch and throw to second base.
- *Cut three* means catch and throw to third base.
- *Cut four* means catch and throw home.

Outfielders chasing down a ball can also help in the communication process by having the player who is not actually fielding the ball look to the infield, anticipate the play, and yell to his fellow outfielder where he should throw. This is especially important on relay plays.

❑ The Cutoff System

In Figure 6-4, the ball has been hit to the right of the cutoff line, so the cutoff is the first baseman's job. Note how the middle infielders adjust by covering second. If the ball is hit to the right, then the shortstop covers second; the second baseman should cover if the ball is hit to the left of second. The middle infielder, on whose side the ball has been hit, chases out to play a rebound if the outfielder makes an error, or to anticipate the relay play if the outfielder misses the ball altogether.

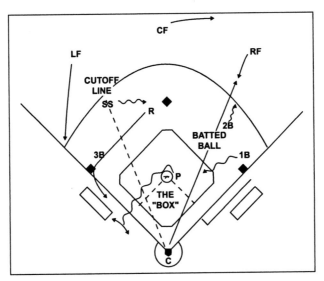

Figure 6-4

The left fielder and center fielder have backup responsibilities, too, as illustrated in Figure 6-4. In this play, the left fielder is anticipating an overthrow at third from either the first baseman or the catcher, who might become involved in a rundown if the runner gets hung up between third and home, which is common at this level of baseball.

❏ *Cutoff Plays*

In Figure 6-5, note how the first baseman works his way into the infield. If the ball were to skip past or rebound off the left fielder, it might enable him to have enough time to serve as the cutoff man. If he can get there, he simply calls off the third baseman, who then covers third, releasing the shortstop from potential relay or rundown duty. You should always have your first baseman to be the cutoff man because it ensures a degree of consistency.

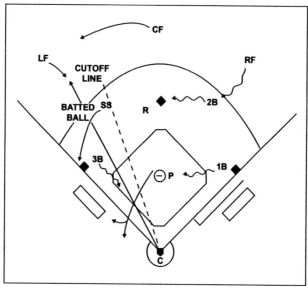

Figure 6-5

The Relay System

If the ball has been hit deeply into the gap, down the line, or it has been misplayed by the outfielder, you're now looking at his jersey number as he chases the ball. At this point more than just a cutoff is needed.

A simple system for relays calls for the field to be divided in half—right up the middle, as shown in Figure 6-6. On any ball hit to the right side, the second baseman runs out for the relay. On any ball hit to the left side, the shortstop takes the relay throw. The middle infielder covers second. This is an old baseball standard—simple and sound. Effectively executed, you get the ball back into the infield—even to the tag point—in two throws.

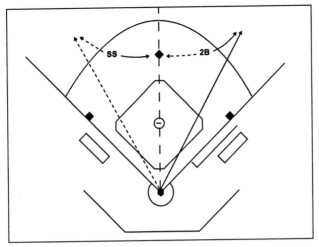

Figure 6-6

The following are additional tactics for the Cutoff and Relay Systems:

- Shortstop cutoff with a pop-up behind first: When a runner is in scoring position and the batter skies a pop-up behind first, the only player who can act as the cutoff is the shortstop. Think about it—the first baseman, second baseman, and right fielder are all converging on the ball. Someone has to throw the runner out and it's a hurried play. The shortstop can get there—remember Derek Jeter's remarkable play for the Yankees in the 2001 playoffs? This coverage is what got him there.

- Some coaches prefer the added insurance of a *double cutoff*. In this play, you send the shortstop to the outfield trailed by the second baseman if the ball is hit into the left-field gap. Conversely, send the second baseman trailed by the shortstop if

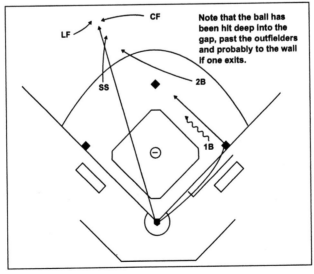

Figure 6-7

the ball is hit into the right-center gap. Remember that the first baseman is trailing the play. The advantage of the double-cutoff system (illustrated in Figure 6-7) is that it provides backup on a missed or overthrown cutoff throw. Note that the ball has been hit deep into the gap past the outfielders, probably to the wall if one exists. The double-cutoff play can also be used for balls hit down the lines, but it obviously entails a long run for the trailing middle infielder.

• In the cutoff play to third base, either the shortstop (Figure 6-8) or the first baseman (Figure 6-9) can take the throw.

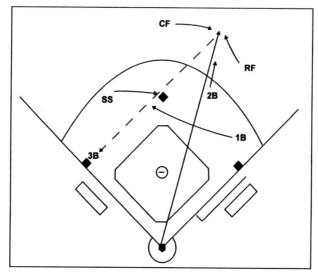

Figure 6-8. Third-base cutoff play. Shortstop takes the throw

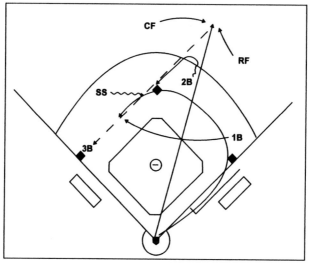

Figure 6-9. Third-base cutoff play. First baseman takes the throw.

The only time you'd use the first baseman as a cutoff man to third is on a ball hit deep to the right side. In this case the shortstop covers second and the second baseman commits to the outfield for a relay.

If the shortstop is being used for the cutoff, the second baseman is only a decoy. He'll react by moving into the outfield and then circle back to cover second in case the runner takes a wide turn. The shortstop sets up in line for a throw to third or back to second. If the ball is hit into the right-center gap, the shortstop also goes out, in this case as part of the normal relay system.

One thing remains to be said concerning when outfielders can *throw through* directly to a base. Any of the three outfielders can throw directly to second for an out, and the corner outfielders can throw through to their corner base (i.e., left fielder to third and right fielder to first). They can also throw directly home when inside the 20-foot rule perimeter (i.e., 20 feet off the edge of the infield dirt). Otherwise, the rule is always to hit the cutoff or relay man in the nose with the baseball, figuratively speaking. Some coaches prefer to say it this way: "If you're going to miss the cutoff man, miss high," especially if you use the double-cut system.

First-and-Third Defense

Defending against the double steal is just as important as utilizing it on the attack. You should select three of the following defenses for your team to focus on, then add one or two more if time and sophistication permit. All of the defenses described in this section begin with your middle infielders at *double-play depth*.

The Optional Cut

Against the double–steal illustrated in Figure 6-10, the shortstop covers second, and the third baseman holds the runner on third. The critical play comes from the second baseman. On the break by the runner on first, he darts into a position directly on line between home and second, facing the runner leading off third. If that runner goes, the second baseman cuts the throw and fires home. If the runner holds at third, he lets the throw go through to second where it's handled by the shortstop for a tag play or rundown.

If the runner is dancing off third, and a quick throw may pick him off—then do it. Or if the runner is caught so far off the bag that the second baseman can catch the throw, run at him, and set up a rundown—then do it. Remember that the runner off third is a primary out, so picking him off always has the highest priority. Also, any fielder running at a runner to chase him back to the bag must run at an angle toward the advance base and cut him off, as illustrated in Figure 6-11.

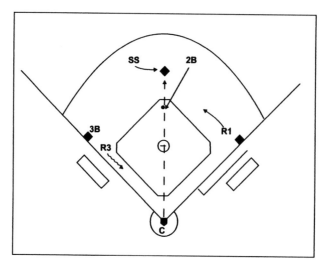

Figure 6-10. Optional cut

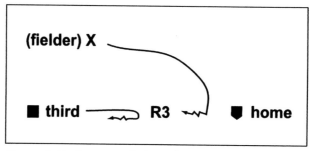

Figure 6-11. Proper technique for cutting off a runner

Many times your defense will trap the runner between first and second bases in a rundown. The infielders involved should focus their attention on the trapped runner and not sneak glances at third. Control of the runner off third is in the hands of the catcher and/or the coaches, who must call, "Four," if the runner breaks for home. The infielder with the ball, no matter how close he is to tagging the back runner, must wheel and fire home.

Here's the caveat: if you tell the fielders to *get an out,* it means game conditions have changed and the normal priority of getting the runner on third is no longer pressing—you would rather trade a run for getting an out in the field.

You could also use a *three* call that means the runner on third hasn't broken for home, but has strayed off the bag too far and is in the vulnerable *gray area.* Upon hearing this call, the fielder with the ball is instructed not to throw immediately to third base; he should merely check the runner and either throw to third, throw home, or run at the base runner, depending on what he sees.

The catcher's role in this defense needs more elaboration. He must initially check the runner on third as he steps to throw to second. This is done either to hold the runner or pick him off with a quick throw if he's caught off the base. Coaches on this level need to be aware that too many catchers want to throw the ball right at the second baseman or even lob the ball so that it can be cut off.

Insist upon a strong throw to second, ignoring all runners once the catcher has made the decision to throw through. Since many catchers have weak arms in youth baseball, you can allow a line-drive *skip* throw, like shortstop Ozzie Smith used to make across Astroturf infields. It's better that a *balloon throw* that could be overthrown.

Middle infielders involved in the rundown between first and second should literally walk the runner back toward first base. In this way, they are under control and can quickly adjust to throw the ball home if they hear the *four* call, and since many third-base runners will try to match the infielder step-for-step as part of their reads off third, walking the runner back creates a false key.

The Return-Throw Defense

This defense is safer and easier to execute, but it does allow the opposition to steal second. In Figure 6-12, both middle infielders cut toward second base, but after two steps, the shortstop plants and drives toward home. The catcher doesn't look the runner back. This factor, as well as the angle of the throw, hopefully creates a throw-through steal read. You want the runner to break for home. The shortstop receives the ball and reacts to the runner. He may simply have to *eat* the ball if the runner hasn't taken the bait. Coaches should look at the runner on third before calling this play. If he's dancing off the bag and itching to go, call it and nail him.

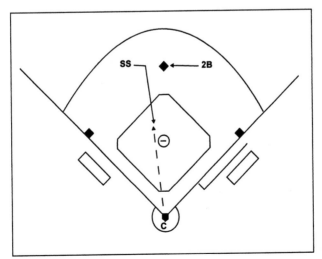

Figure 6-12. The return-throw defense

Supplemental First-and-Third Defenses

The Yankee Pick

Back when Buck Showalter was managing the New York Yankees, they used a defense that was safe and, on occasion, produced a cheap out. Before any runner has broken and the pitcher has reached his set position, he steps off the rubber, vigorously pumps a fake throw to third, and then wheels and fires to first base. The runner off first is often caught leaning or even breaking late.

Fake Throw-Through

Another safe defense (but admittedly low on the scale of effectiveness) is to have the catcher pump fake a throw to second and then fire to third if the runner is leaning. He can also throw through to the pitcher who can snap a throw to third. Both moves require a solid pump fake—no *short-armers*—to make the runner bite on the fake. Some coaches even ask the catcher to grunt to draw the runner. Other coaches have the pitcher exaggerate his follow-through, and have the catcher throw to a spot where his head was. This makes the throw look as if it's going to second base.

Defending the Off-the-Pitcher Play

Occasionally the offense dictates your defense. If the enemy opts to run a delayed steal off the pitcher or catcher (as described in Chapter 5), you should train your pitchers to use one set response. Have them step off the rubber (behind it), check the runner on third (snap throw if you have him), wheel, and fire to the second baseman, who has charged directly in from his normal position. He should be standing on the baseline about 10 to 15 feet from the bag to cut off the runner. The middle infielders then proceed to trap this runner with an ear to the catcher for a possible *four* call.

This should be the pitcher's only move. He should not be allowed to run around, dance about, or act confused. His response is always the same so that it becomes automatic, minimizing the chance for errors.

Defending the Dropped Third-Strike Steal

Have the first baseman come up the line toward home, receive a short throw, and tag the runner who's just hit the ball. From this position he can easily throw out a runner attempting to steal home. To add extra insurance, circle the second baseman around to cover first to back up the throw.

This whole system does take practice, but it can be incorporated into general situation practices. Even if you spend just 20 minutes a week on your double-steal defenses, it can bring significant rewards in the win-loss column.

Holding Runners at Second Base

Given the aggressiveness of base runners at this level, it's imperative to hold runners leading off second, to keep them close and hinder their attempts to steal. You can use a series of four verbal signals. The call is based upon hitting tendencies and whether the hitter is a lefty or righty. The pitcher's fastball velocity factors in, too.

The first two calls involve the shortstop or the second baseman holding the runner on second by standing one stride away from the bag. The fielder must keep his body weight on the foot nearest the bag and push off that foot to scramble back toward his defensive position when the pitcher delivers home. The infielder not involved in the call plays his normal depth.

Figure 6-13 illustrates a *40 hold* where the second baseman holds the runner, and *60 hold* where the shortstop holds the runner. These calls are not pickoff plays, although the pitcher can throw over if he feels the need. To recover their defensive positions, the infielders take a flatter and shallower route to gain a better angle and cover more infield.

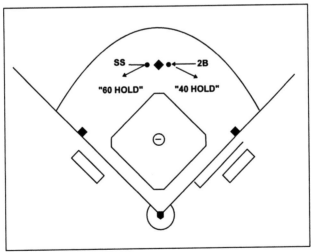

Figure 6-13. 40 hold and 60 hold

The next two calls are slightly more elaborate and are intended to make the runner think that a pickoff play may be coming. You would call out a *46* or a *64* depending on the tendencies of the hitters. In calling these coverages, *4* and *6* are numbers assigned to fielders in a conventional scoring system. Therefore, if you call *46*, you want the second baseman (the first numbered position called) to dart within a step of the bag and then fade back to recover his defensive position. As soon as he begins his fade, the shortstop darts to the bag, again to a position within one step of the base. All of this movement, which is called *flashing*, distracts the runner and maybe even the coach.

Figure 6-14 illustrates a *46* call; a *64* call is the mirror opposite. The problem is that one infielder will be caught out of position, but it's a calculated and necessary risk.

All of this occurs when the pitcher comes to the set position. He's responsible for at least looking the runner back, perhaps stepping off behind the rubber—whatever he can do to keep the runner guessing and off his maximum lead.

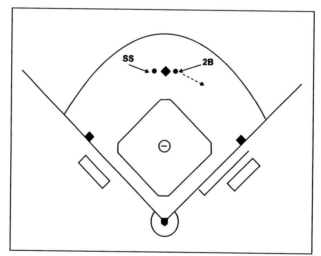

Figure 6-14. 46 call

As a wrinkle, you can also use a *pinch* call in which both middle infielders simultaneously dart toward the bag from double-play depth (where all of these coverages initially originate) to a position halfway to the base. They then slide back to recover their defensive alignments.

Pickoff Plays

Pickoff plays are one of those elements of baseball that make the game fun. Remember, calling for a pickoff play doesn't actually have to produce an out for it to be effective. You might want to call at least one pickoff play early in a game to show your opponent that you have it in your arsenal. This way you create doubt, hesitation, and caution right off the bat! Once they've seen it, opposition runners may shorten their leads or be a step more cautious. And if you succeed in picking off a runner, you've stolen the momentum of the game.

The following are three pickoff plays for you to incorporate into your game strategy throughout the season. You should always use a verbal signal to call pickoffs, most often with a selected key word followed by the first name or nickname of the infielder who will be receiving the pickoff throw.

First Base: The Circle-In Pickoff

In the circle-in pickoff (illustrated in Figure 6-15), the first baseman releases from holding the runner and slips toward home as if covering a bunt. This allows the runner to expand his lead and hopefully distract him (and his coach) from seeing the second baseman circling in behind him to cover first. The pitcher throws a pitchout, and then the catcher fires to first. He may have to improvise by throwing to second (where the shortstop is covering) if the runner has broken on the pitch. Be sure to initiate the play's movement with a loud call of, "Watch the bunt!"

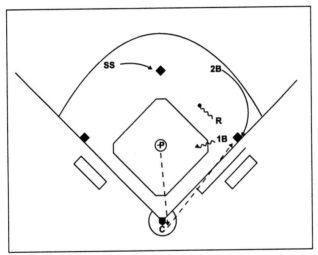

Figure 6-15. The circle-in pickoff

Remember to have your pitchers practice pitchouts, as these throws are unnatural and often elicit wild air balls. Be aware there's a downside to this play: that it's difficult for the catcher to throw a runner out at second, even with a pitchout, because of the big lead you've allowed.

Most teams will run a play like this with the first baseman darting in. He will play behind the runner, especially if two men are on base and you need a third out. Upon a prearranged signal between the pitcher and catcher or even just between the first baseman and pitcher, he cuts in behind the runner and receives a throw from either the catcher or the pitcher. The problem is that you are throwing behind a runner, so use this only when a third out is assured from an over-aggressive runner leading off first. To differentiate this play, you may wish to refer to it as the *cut in* pickoff.

Second Base: The Zigzag Pickoff

Widen the second baseman outward to build a false sense of security for the runner leading off second. The pitcher sets, looks once at the runner, and never again looks back. The pick has been called, and the shortstop darts toward the runner, not the base, as shown in Figure 6-16. He then backpedals straight back, taking three steps, as if returning to his defensive position. Once he starts back, the catcher flashes the pickoff sign (five fingers), and the pitcher uses a leg-lift motion as if he were going home; instead he spins and fires to second. (Luis Tiant often used this pickoff move.)

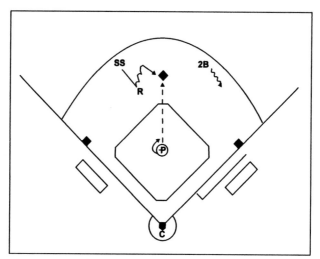

Figure 6-16. The zigzag pickoff

You should coordinate with the infielders. After the shortstop takes three steps, he breaks for the bag, receives the throw, and applies the tag. The center fielder provides backup. For this play to be successful, your pitchers must work on their spin (Tiant) move.

Second Base: The Shadow Pickoff

The name *shadow pickoff* derives from the shortstop's role. The pitcher uses the same spin move as in the zigzag pickoff and coordinates with the catcher's sign in the same way. Both infielders play at double-play depth.

The play begins with the third baseman slipping in as if giving up the bag to cover a bunt, as shown in Figure 6-17. The shortstop circles around in front of the runner, skips in front of him when his line of sight to the pitcher is blocked, and then the shortstop obnoxiously slaps his glove. The catcher flashes five fingers at this point, and the second baseman darts in to take the throw.

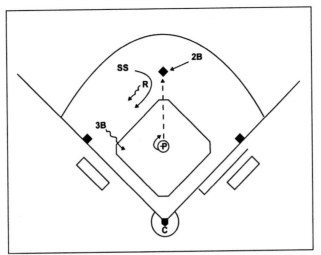

Figure 6-17. The shadow pickoff

Be sure your shortstop remains *on the baseline edge of the grass* so he doesn't interfere with the runner. Also make sure the third baseman doesn't dance in too far; he should be only about five feet in on the grass, just enough to make the runner expand his lead. Since this pickoff play usually creates a rundown, the third baseman must be able to recover his position.

Third Base: The Cumberland Pick

Cumberland County College used this one. With a runner leading off third, have the third baseman slide to his left and the catcher skip a hard throw past him, as if it was an errant throw. The runner should break off third, but your shortstop, knowing what's on, has broken to his right to back up the throw. He fields it and throws the runner out. Keep in mind that the pitcher must throw a pitchout to initiate this called play.

Bunt Defenses

No Runner on Base

When the batter lays down a bunt, or even shows bunt, the corner infielders and pitcher *automatically* charge the plate while the second baseman sprints to cover first and the shortstop moves to cover second, as shown in Figure 6-18. The only part of this play that can lead to confusion is the *tweener*—a bunt that slides between the first baseman and the pitcher, usually on the right side. Communication is fundamental on this play. The calls of "I got the ball!" and "I got the base!" are necessary. The player who doesn't get the ball must cover the base. It might be necessary to make another base call if two infielders like the pitcher and second baseman converge on the bag. Teach this in situation and in drills where you hit fungoes into the right side *tweener zone.*

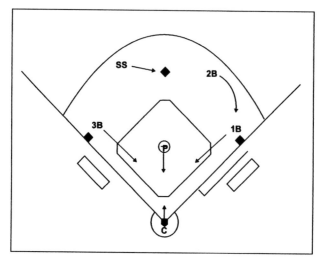

Figure 6-18. Normal bunt coverage with no one on base or only a runner on first

Runner on First

This defense operates the same way as the previous one, but with an additional requirement. If the ball is bunted to the left side (see Figure 6-19), the pitcher may have to cover third if the third baseman is fielding the ball. The *I got the base* and *I got the ball* calls work again here. A heads-up runner will take third if it's vacant, so be sure third is covered by either the pitcher racing across or the third baseman backpedaling.

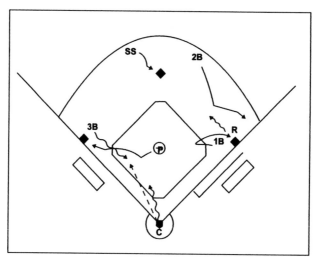

Figure 6-19. Runner on first, ball bunted to left side

Runner on Second

In the *rotation play* often used in the pros, the third baseman charges when the batter shows bunt, and the shortstop rotates over to cover third, as shown in Figure 6-20. However, on this level the play often becomes a footrace between the runner and the shortstop. In addition, asking the harried shortstop to catch a throw and apply a tag—all in motion—may be too much for him.

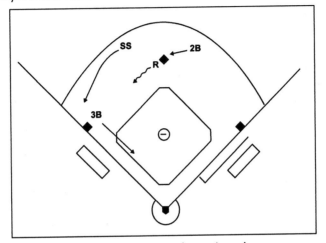

Figure 6-20. Runner on second, rotation play

Instead of using the rotation play, hold the third baseman for third base coverage (as shown in Figure 6-21) and remind the pitcher that it's his responsibility to get all bunts on the left side. Caution the first baseman that he may have a very difficult play coming up. Since there's no force play, the pitcher needs to check the runner off second and snap throw to first. An aggressive runner may break for third after the throw, necessitating a throw from first to third—the least-worked-on throw in baseball. A good wrinkle here is to allow the pitcher to pump fake either to pick the runner off or to hold him, if he senses that the runner may break for third after his throw.

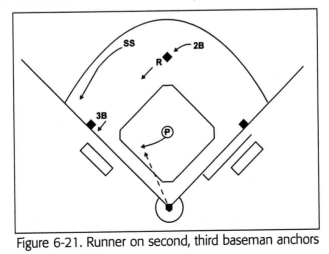

Figure 6-21. Runner on second, third baseman anchors

Runners on First and Second

The same defensive principles cited previously apply here—rotation or anchoring the third baseman. The only thing to add is that it's crucial for the pitcher to throw out the lead runner at third. There's no need to check him, and the force play makes it a safer and easier play.

Runner on Third

Since the third baseman is charging on this play (probably a squeeze play), the shortstop must rotate over to cover third, as shown in Figure 6-22. As mentioned in Chapter 5, you have two types of squeeze plays to choose from: safety and suicide. A safety squeeze calls for the runner on third to break for home only when the ball has made contact with the bat. On the suicide squeeze, the runner breaks for home on the delivery of the pitch. He hopes for the best as he steals home.

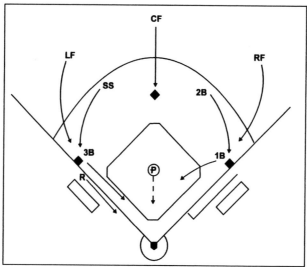

Figure 6-22. Bunt defense with runner on third

To defend against the suicide plays, have the third baseman hold the runner at third with his right foot set on the inside corner of the bag. Don't allow him to straddle as it inhibits mobility. The pitcher must throw over to third at least once, even if it's a calling card. If the batter squares, both corner infielders as well as the pitcher charge. If the batter squares to bunt and the runner on third breaks for home, the third baseman sprints for home right alongside him. The shortstop covers third, and the second baseman covers first. The center fielder, reading the play, covers second. The right fielder and left fielder back up first and third, respectively.

If the pitcher reads the suicide squeeze and can make a target adjustment with his pitch, some coaches have him throw at the batter's head or groin to back him off the plate. You might want to recommend a more benign target, such as a pitch up and in, high in the strike zone, to create a pop-up.

Realize that a well-executed suicide squeeze is virtually unstoppable no matter how well you defend it. You do have a shot at home if the opposing coach has called the squeeze with bases loaded, but generally speaking, it's imperative that all bases are covered and you seek an out elsewhere. Communication is vital in this regard. Look for trailing runners who might try to stretch their run or have taken too big a turn around their base.

CHAPTER 7

Positional Fundamentals

Positional Practices

Sometime during the preseason, you'll need to call a few brief instructional practices to review esoteric fundamentals relevant to each position. It's recommended to do this during the first week of practice and call for any and all players who are even thinking about coming out for a particular position on the team. Once you've taught this material in the preseason, try to work these skills at least once per week in positional practices during the season.

Infielders

Fielding techniques

❏ Alligator chop

All infielders must be taught the standard *alligator chop* technique employed in fielding grounders. Note the following in Figure 7-1:

- The fielder is squared to the ball (midline the ball).
- The foot on the throwing-hand side is slightly back.
- The top hand traps the ball from on top.
- The fielder flexes at the knees as well as the hips.
- The fielder looks the ball into the glove.

Figure 7-1. Alligator chop

❑ Backhand

All infielders also need to learn the proper backhand technique, which consists of two key steps. First, the player plants his foot and stabs his glove to stop the ball, as shown in Figure 7-2. Then, he pivots, wheels, and fires the ball, as illustrated in Figure 7-3.

Figure 7-2. Backhand technique—plant and stab

Figure 7-3. Backhand technique—pivot, wheel, and fire

❑ Crow Hop

Receive the ball at arm's length and with two hands. Pivot the foot on the throwing-hand side to the outside, pull up to a semi-tuck position, and snap throw. Keep the hands high at all times for quicker release. See Figure 7-4.

Figure 7-4. Crow hop fielding technique

❑ Relay throw

In the relay throw technique, the player gives target, then once the ball is in the air, he turns and catches the ball across his body, with the glove side toward the target. Finally, he takes one step toward the target as he loads up to throw. See Figure 7-5.

Figure 7-5. Relay throw

Infield Footwork

Proper footwork is as important as proper catching and throwing technique. Young ballplayers need to be taught the following steps. You should incorporate them all into your daily agility drills.

❑ Prepitch Movement

Prepitch *dance steps* keep the athlete from being caught flat-footed. The infielder begins with the weight on the balls of his feet, preferably the inside edge. He must take two steps and then land with both feet balanced and spread at the point the pitched ball reaches the hitting zone. The prepitch sequence can actually begin off either foot since the athlete arrives balanced and squared up at the point of contact. (See Figure 7-6.)

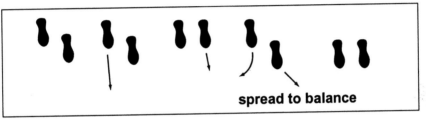

spread to balance

Figure 7-6. Pre-pitch movement

❑ The Shuffle-Glide

After fielding a ground ball, teach the shuffle-glide. The fielder steps toward the target, replacing one foot with the other, without crossing over, as shown in Figure 7-7.

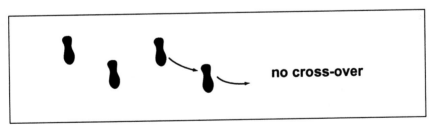

no cross-over

Figure 7-7. Shuffle-glide

First Basemen

Receiving Throws

You should cover throws inside the bag, to the outfield side of the bag, dirt balls, high throws, and stretch plays. Some of the fundamentals include the following:

- Come off the bag immediately on a ball thrown inside the bag and make a sweep tag on the runner (never stretch for this ball).

- Stretch for a ball on the outfield side of the bag only if the dead ball fence is close.

- Leap from the bag on high throws to get an extra two to three inches and come back down on the top of the bag.

- Never stretch too early and avoid locking yourself on plays you know will be close.

- Explode out to the ball as it reaches your glove.

- Keep the foot on the throwing-hand side of the bag for all throw receptions.

Holding Runners

Set the right foot on the corner and side of the bag facing toward third and home. The reason is simple: on a wide pickoff throw from the pitcher that sails to the second base or upfield side of the base, the first baseman can leap to catch it by springing toward second rather than straddling the bag and getting tied up with the runner. Always sweep the tag toward the back-inside edge of the bag. Players at this age tend to tag runners high. Discourage this because any upper-body tag allows the argument that the feet are in safely ahead of the tag.

Relay Throws

Fielders should cover relay throws as well as slow-rollers and bunt-coverage fundamentals as part of a group. Defending the *dropped third strike with a runner on* has special implications for the first baseman, which has been covered in the section on first-and-third defenses in Chapter 6. There's also infield group work. With all this practice, no special instruction is needed—just remind them.

Middle Infielders

Double-Play Pivots and Feeds

Shortstop Feed

Work on the shovel throw where the shortstop stays low, drops the right knee as it pivots toward second, and shovels the ball over to the second baseman. (See Figure 7-8.) You also need to work the backhand catch as well as the backhand feed. On the backhand catch (which transcends double-play pivots and can be utilized in any infield setting), teach them to stab the ball with the glove opened to the backhand with the near foot planted. Then they take one crossover step to wheel and fire across to first or second base. Drill this with soft toss initially, and verbally choreograph it by calling out, "One, two, pivot, throw!"

Figure 7-8. Shortstop's shovel feed

Second Baseman's Feed

The knee-drop technique is often used when the throw must travel from normal depth (see Figure 7-9). The second baseman must also be taught the backhand toss, which is used when he's in close. Pushed away from the body with little or no rotation on the ball, this throw replicates a quarterback pitching a football on the option play with the thumb rotated downward and the open palm pointed to the receiver.

Figure 7-9. Second baseman's knee-drop toss

Also teach the hop-turn feed, which is used from a distance when some strength is needed for a throw. The hop-turn feed involves jumping from the fielding stance, and placing both feet into throwing position simultaneously.

Shortstop Double-Play Pivot

An element of timing is required in this play. You should ask the shortstop to stutter-step his feet so he'll arrive at the bag just as the throw does. He's instructed to straddle the back corner of the bag (center field side) with his left foot in the lead, as shown in Figure 7-10. The hands are extended and as the ball is caught, he drags his right toe (the trailing foot) over the corner of the base. He's supposed to catch the ball, pull it with both hands toward the throwing hand shoulder, and snap a throw to first base—always moving toward first in one continuous fluid motion.

Figure 7-10. Shortstop double-play pivot

You can use two techniques to teach this. The first one is to have the pivot man, shortstop, or second baseman catch the ball with a paddle glove or the closed back of the regular fielder's glove to ensure his use of both hands. For the second one, lie on the ground and swing your fungo bat like a metronome across the base to teach them to clear the baseline and avoid an incoming sliding runner.

Second Baseman Double-Play Pivots

There's an old story about how a major league team brought nine all-star second basemen to spring training one year, and they ended up teaching nine different double-play pivots! The point is that the pivot as executed by the second baseman is a matter of creativity and comfort—do what works best for you. However, since you're dealing with young ballplayers, it's best to teach them one standard pivot that works for everyone and gets the job done efficiently.

Figure 7-11 illustrates a drill for working both pivots and feeds. The coach is in the middle and feeds grounders to the shortstop or second baseman. They toss to the pivot man, who then fires to first. Work the ground-ball feeds at various angles to the right and left of the shortstop or second baseman. If you wish to swing a bat over the bag as described earlier, use a player to feed the balls, but don't use a player to swing the distraction bat as injuries can result.

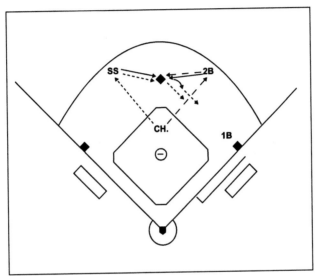

Figure 7-11. Double-play pivot drill

In Figure 7-12, the second baseman has set up to receive the throw with his hands properly extended and target presented. His right foot is on the edge of the bag and ready to push off when he receives the throw. Note how he clears the base path in Figure 7-13. You shouldn't teach the foot-drag method described for the shortstop because it forces the pivot man's momentum away from first. Arm strength being what it is on this level, the kids need every advantage they can get.

Relay throws and rundowns

These are taught and drilled as a group at other times, but they certainly can be addressed during positional practice.

Short-hop catches

Since all players need to be adept at short-hop catches, you may prefer to teach them as a team drill during the preseason.

On a ball thrown at their feet, the natural instinct is to turn the head away and sweep the glove at the ball, hoping for the best in terms of a catch. Players must overcome this and react to the dirt ball by setting their glove at the point where the ball will short-hop into it. They learn this only by repetition. A good drill to practice is called the *short-hop catch*. Set the players in pairs about 20 feet apart and tell them to throw the ball—with force—directly at their partner's feet. At first they'll want to bounce it softly somewhere in between each other. Insist on hard, challenging throws.

Figure 7-12. Second baseman's double-play pivot, part one

Figure 7-13. Second baseman's double-play pivot, part two

Slow-rollers

Have players charge the ball, but apply this rule: if the ball is rolling, glove it; if it's dead, pick it up barehanded. When catching barehanded, reach down with the fingers extended into a throwing grip right away and stab the ball into the ground. The foot on the bare-hand side should be nearest the ball and serve as the pivot for the throw. If the ball is rolling slightly and it is a do-or-die situation, have the fielder scoop under the ball with the fingers pre-set in a throwing position.

Third Basemen

The positional package for third basemen includes much of what is taught as fundamental to the other infielders—but there are two other areas to stress:

- Slow rollers and the throw-on-the-run technique: Admittedly a very difficult play for kids at this level, it must be drilled and taught for their future development.

- Cutting across the face of the shortstop: Young third basemen assigned to the proverbial *hot corner* must be taught this play.

Set your shortstop, third baseman, and a receiver at first in normal infield position. Then fungo everything from high hoppers to slow rollers to ground smashes (a.k.a. *worm burners*). Have the third baseman get to everything he can by reading the angle, gathering his feet, and making a crisp, accurate throw to first. Rarely will the third baseman angle back toward shortstop on this play; he must cut across the shortstop's position, usually on the grass.

After working on these skills, teach your third basemen how to backhand the hard smash over the bag. Many coaches now teach the knee-drop technique with the left knee and a snapped pickup on the backhand over and behind the bag. Teach this with short toss and evolve to fungoes. Some coaches also teach a slide-and-recovery technique.

Outfielders

Rounding

A ground ball—even one that's hard hit—must never be allowed to skip past and between two outfielders or even down the line. Teach outfielders to go back on the ball and approach it coming in on line with their intended throw target. The diagram in Figure 7-14 illustrates this. It must be drilled to both sides, so use the *ball in the gap* drill, illustrated in Figure 7-15. This drill can also be used for fly balls.

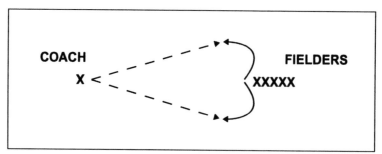

Figure 7-14. Rounding principle for grounders

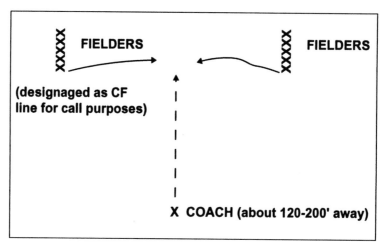

Figure 7-15. Ball-in-the-gap drill

Designate one line of players as the center fielder, who has primary call responsibilities, and then fungo fly balls and grounders between them. You may wish to isolate the ground ball rounding technique with only one line of outfielders and work them to either side.

Sliding Catches

Outfielders must be taught to overcome their fear of sliding to catch fly balls. In teaching them to make the sliding catch, you should line them up about 25 feet away from a coach who's throwing soft pop-ups into the air. The fielders must time it so they arrive late and make a simple bent-leg slide to come up with the ball.

Many great catches that you see on the sports highlight shows on TV are headlong dives. This technique is fine for a ball in the gap, but your primary concern is the *Texas League* blooper with a high trajectory that if missed doesn't travel far past the fielder anyway. So you need to teach your players to go down for the ball.

There are several reasons for the bent-leg slide:

- It's much safer than diving.
- Recovery after the catch is quicker and easier than diving.
- The arms and hands are free to adjust to the ball.

The first body parts to hit the ground in a diving catch are the arms and elbows, thus locking them in. With the bent-leg sliding catch, the legs and fanny are first on the ground, so the arms and hands remain free.

Ball in the Sun

If you're negligent about teaching how to catch a fly ball in the sun (or to slide properly, for that matter), and your players get hurt, lawsuits can occur. When a player gets injured, the first question inevitably asked is: was he taught how to do this properly?

To teach this technique properly, line up the kids facing the sun and have them drop one foot back to get a sideways perspective on the ball; this way the ball comes out of the sun more quickly because of the angle. Simultaneously have them shield the sun with their glove. Look to see if a shadow is cast across the face. Next, drill the outfielders by lining them up and short-tossing pop-ups, just as you did in the sliding-catch drill.

Throwing Out Runners Who Are Tagging Up

Start by lining up the players as in the previous drill. Have the outfielders gauge where the ball will drop and then take a step back from the drop point. Have them angle their approach to the ball by moving in the direction of the intended throw—usually home, third, or to a cutoff man. They must catch the ball with two hands and on their throwing-hand side for quicker release. They should be moving under the ball and toward their target at the precise moment the ball hits the glove. A crow hop and then a hard overhand throw finish the play. Insist that your outfielders never allow themselves to be caught moving back on such a play. They must get behind the ball and move in toward the release point.

Playing the Fence

Most of the fields you play on probably won't have outfield fences. But when you do, your players need to have been taught the skill of *playing the fence*. Also, since most fields do have foul-line fencing, the techniques used to play the ball when it's near a fence need to be taught to corner infielders as well as outfielders.

The rules are simple: go back on the ball using the crossover lateral steps you teach during your daily agility drills, and retreat with the glove toward the ball and the bare hand outstretched toward the fence to feel the wall.

Rather than have them alternately glancing at the wall and the descending ball, allow fielders one look back to the wall as they sense they're approaching it. The remainder of the time they should focus on the ball while feeling for the wall with their hand. Remember that the other outfielder needs to be communicating with his teammate, telling him how much room he has to the fence and where to throw the ball for his next play.

The outstretched-arm technique is also beneficial for two other reasons: the hand can be used to help climb the fence should it be necessary to go up for the ball, and the glove is on the proper side to catch the ball. Drill this by lining up the outfielders against a fence or the backstop. Place one outfielder about 10 feet from the fence and soft-toss pop flies to the base of the wall as they fade back. The next player in line communicates to the player going back toward the fence.

Do or Die

There is a risk in teaching young outfielders the *do-or-die* technique for fear they'll use it too often. It's only appropriate when the runner is attempting to gain an extra base or even score a run on a grounder that has skipped into the outfield. Your outfielders need to charge the ball and throw the runner out. Teach them to attack the ball, with a proper rounding angle at full speed, only throttling down within the last couple of steps. They must approach the ball on the glove side and stab it as the foot on that

Figure 7-16. Outfielder's hard-charge do-or-die technique. The outfielder plants his gloveside foot and keeps his head down to retrieve the ball.

Figure 7-17. Outfielder's hard-charge do-or-die technique. The outfielder crow hops before throwing the ball.

same side is planted near the ball, keeping their head down and looking the ball into the glove, as shown in Figure 7-16. The tendency to look up is fatal because it causes the glove to pick up too early.

It's critical that ball, glove, and near foot are all on the same side. Upon receiving the ball, pull up, and crow hop as shown in Figure 7-17, then fire a strike on the next stride. Two strides after the ball has been caught are all that you allow on this quick charge and throw. Drill it by rolling grounders to players in line. Remember that the technique is totally different for infielders charging a ball, and that this technique is only to be used in *do-or-die* situations because the percentage for error is high. As a final point in coaching your outfielders, don't neglect ground balls in general, as 70 percent of what they catch in a game are grounders.

Coaching Catchers

Catcher's Stances

At this level, you should teach your catchers two basic stances—the comfort stance and the coiled stance. They should use the comfort stance, shown in Figure 7-18, when no one is on base. The coiled stance, illustrated in Figure 7-19, is the proper stance to use with one or more runners on base.

Figure 7-18. Comfort stance (no one on base)

Figure 7-19. Coiled stance (runners on)

Catcher Drills

Volumes have been written on the techniques involved in the art of catching. On this level of baseball, however, a simple drill series presented here is all you'll need to develop your catchers' skills and arm strength. Taken together, these drills should be finished in 15 minutes, 20 at the most. It can be the most valuable time segment of the day. You should do this twice weekly in preseason and once per week during the season.

Drill 1: Framing

Have the catchers squat behind home plate and throw tennis balls at their bare glove hand, which should be placed in the proper receiving position. They're supposed to tilt the hand so that the ball rebounds from their palm onto home plate. No stabbing at the ball is allowed.

You'll also want to ask them to catch and hold the ball as an additional drill. Teach them to open their hand and point their fingers at the pitcher in giving the target and to imagine they're controlling a steering wheel with one hand to frame the pitch. Work both corners, high and low. Also, be sure that the throwing hand is in the proper position, either behind the back or beside the glove, depending upon whether or not a runner is on base.

Drill 2: Dirt Balls

Two drills can be used for dirt balls, one with stationary balls (placed as shown in Figure 7-20) and the other with thrown balls (see Figure 7-21). You might want to use soft-toss rag balls, but certainly suiting up the catchers and using real balls is good practice. Work them laterally as well as directly. Be sure they block balls squarely instead of trying to catch them. They should attack wide balls at an angle toward the pitcher as illustrated in Figure 7-21.

When drilling dirt balls, be sure to include passed balls back to the screen. If your backstop is deep, or if one in an upcoming game is set deep behind home plate, work your catchers on this play. Teach them a pop-up slide to recover the ball and throw a runner out at home. Add the pitchers covering home, too.

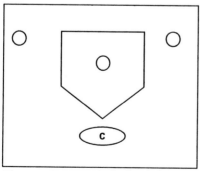

Figure 7-20. Dirt-ball drill with stationary balls

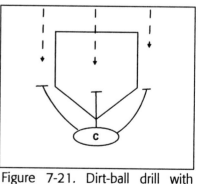

Figure 7-21. Dirt-ball drill with thrown balls

Drill 3: Footwork

Use several home plates if you have them. Have the catchers squat in the stance they use when a runner is on base: offset slightly to their throwing-hand side with the pivot foot open and their butt on an even plane with their knees. You simulate the pitcher's motion and call out, "Going!" as you toss a rag ball to them. They catch and step, cocking the arm with the elbow coming straight up and back to the ear, as if they were going to throw. This is all done in one motion—emphasize quickness. Two hands are a must, as well. Practice the footwork to both second and third bases.

Be sure to have the catchers *close up* to throw. They should tuck their lead shoulder in and toward the target, much like the pitcher closing up on the tuck prior to delivery to the plate. They can facilitate this by bringing the glove up to the throwing-hand shoulder along with the throwing hand itself.

Drill 4: Arm Strength

Set two home plates 120 feet apart (pace out 40 steps). Give each catcher three balls and have him throw from one plate to the other on his knees. Catchers must use proper upper-body twist and quick release. This is difficult for catchers below the high school level. Their tendency is to drop the throwing hand down and throw an air ball. Insist on line-drive throws, even though they will bounce them initially. Their arms will improve as the season progresses.

Drill 5: Pop-Ups

At the beginning of this drill, remind the catchers of two fundamentals:

- Turn away from the batter as you locate the ball. Any pop-up foul is most easily sighted by turning over the shoulder away from the hitter (i.e. for a right-handed batter, the catcher turns over his right shoulder).

- Locate the ball before throwing the mask away.

Now drill from the crouch with mask on. Hit tennis balls high into the air using a tennis racket for good loft and have the catchers run them down.

Normal Catcher Duties

The following are part of the catcher's normal duties:

- Gives signals on every pitch.
- Hides signals properly.
- Provides a good target in the correct location.

- Knows the verbal signal for pitchouts and curves.
- Is aware of the set-up points for the breaking ball and the 0-2 pitch.
- Knows his responsibilities for pickoffs and first-and-third defenses.

Catcher Techniques

Dirt-ball blocking technique

See Figure 7-22.

Figure 7-22. Dirt-ball blocking technique   Figure 7-23. Giving signals

Giving Signals

The catcher aims his right knee at the first baseman to hide the signs from the first base coach. He covers the left side with the glove below the knee, as shown in Figure 7-23.

Closing Up to Throw to Second

Note how the front foot and front shoulder are tucked inward in Figure 7-24 to create a stronger throw by creating good upper body rotation.

Figure 7-24. Closing up to throw to second

Applying the Tag

Block half of the plate by placing the left heel on the corner of home plate that aligns with third base, as shown in Figure 7-25. Upon receipt of the throw, collapse the right leg and *curl* into the tag, effectively blocking the entire plate, as illustrated in Figure 7-26.

Figure 7-25   Figure 7-26

CHAPTER 8

Conditioning and Drills

Creative Conditioning

Your players need conditioning and inevitably it becomes drudgery. But with a little imagination on your part and positive encouragement, even post-practice conditioning can be a palatable learning experience. Teach and drill while you work on aerobic conditioning levels.

Read-and-Steal Sprints

Line up the players along the first base line from the base back into the outfield. You stand on the mound acting as the pitcher. Have them sprint to second base when they read you. They must read the right-hander by keying the back heel once the front foot picks up. Then have them read the lefty with a *toe read, head read,* and *front-knee read.* Conclude with a *gamble* read. (All of these reads were discussed in Chapter 5.) Five reads means five sprints. If one player blows the read or if a runner doesn't sprint all out, then the entire line goes again.

Second-to-Home Sprints

Line up the players by second base, not more than five at a time. Serving as pitcher, you pretend to set and deliver a pitch to the plate. Players step off base along an imaginary line extending from the first to second baseline into the outfield. The players take their primary and secondary leads (at least one-third of the way toward third base) and sprint for home when you say, "Go!" Rather than collide, they're allowed to miss third base in this sprint. Have them all do at least three good sprints.

Running-Rules Sprints

Again you're the pitcher, but this time you have a bag of balls on the mound. The entire team is divided into four groups: one at each base and home. When you deliver an imaginary pitch, finish it off in one of the following ways: roll a ball somewhere in the infield to simulate a grounder that they must read; hold your arm straight out into the air and point toward a particular outfield spot; or hold the ball straight back, simulating a line drive. Since you've taught specific reads for each kind of batted ball, the runners on second and third must read and react properly. The runners going from home to first must either sprint through the bag or round it, depending on whether they read a grounder or fly ball. The runners going from first to second are on a steal read. You could assign ten bases, meaning ten reads or two-and-a-half times around the diamond. Poor reads and players who *dog* around the bases negate the sprint for the entire team.

Passed-Ball Sprints

Set up two lines of players: one near the plate and the other near third. One player at home and one off third will read and sprint simultaneously. Once again, you're on the mound with the ball bag pitching to your assistant coach at the plate. He'll either catch it or miss it depending upon whether or not you throw a wild pitch. If he misses the ball, then the players run to first reading a dropped third strike or from third to home reading a passed ball. (Players coming from Little League, where a strike is a strike, often forget about reading a dropped third strike.)

First-to-Third Sprints

This is the most grueling of the series. Players jog to first and round it with a proper fly ball read angle. They must sprint from first to third touching each base, then walk home. As a coach, you may wish to stand in the first base line about three-quarters of the way down the line to force them around you into a good rounding angle. Encourage hollering and team exhortations in these sprints to motivate players through your toughest conditioner.

Use this drill at least once a week because of the conditioning it provides. You can also use this one when you're concerned about your team's mental focus and concentration. You should write down the mental mistakes and assign one first-to-third sprint for each mental error—loudly calling them out for each team sprint.

The Monday Mile

Baseball players, especially pitchers, need long-distance conditioning for their legs. Each practice week should begin with a dreaded *Monday mile*. You should jog with them, too. It helps boost team morale. Be creative by assigning a perimeter of the fence or a lap around the school—whatever it takes to finish a mile.

Mile runs are also assigned for being late to practice, detention in school, or a request for discipline from a teacher. Here's one cautionary note about running for disciplinary purposes: parents may view this as inappropriate punishment, so it's best to group your miscreant players for the punishment mile, and run with them. As you run, talk baseball with them, so a subtle yet effective message is sent, and potentially critical parents are disarmed.

The day after pitchers have thrown a full game, they must rest their arms while teammates throw in prepractice, so have them run instead. Call it a *pitcher's mile*.

Line-to-Line Sprints

Assign these during a scrimmage or before a game when you want to be sure the team is well conditioned and ready to play. Players should sprint from the right field foul line to center field, and then from center field to the left field foul line, and back again. They can go by themselves or with friends, but they must do them. Since this conditioning needs no direct supervision, it's convenient when you're tied up with other coaching duties.

Sequence Sprints

Have the players complete the following sequence:

- Sprint from home to first and jog back.
- Sprint from home to third and jog in.
- Sprint from home to second.
- Sprint from second to home.
- Sprint around the bases.

Hustle Sprints

Line up the kids at the edge of the dugout. Each player or pair of players gets a designated number corresponding to the numbers assigned to positions used in scoring baseball games (pitcher = 1, catcher =2, first baseman = 3, etc.). On the whistle, they are to sprint to their assigned spot on the field. On the next whistle, they jog back to the dugout and get reassigned another number and position based on a prescribed rotation.

Stationary Bike

Some coaches may be reluctant to offer their players a running program and prefer stationary bicycling to enhance aerobic conditioning. The following is an excellent stationary bike program used by the Philadelphia Flyers of the National Hockey League.

Phase 1: 20-minute workout

- 4 minutes at 70 rpm
- 1 minute at 110 rpm
- Repeat four times

Phase 2: 21-minute workout

- 8 minutes at 90 rpm as a warm-up
- 3 sets of 45 seconds at 100 rpm
- 90 seconds at 70 rpm
- 2 sets of 30 seconds at 100 rpm
- 1 minute at 70 rpm
- 75 seconds at 100 rpm
- 1 minute at 70 rpm
- 30 seconds at 100 rpm
- 1 minute at 70 rpm as cool-down.

Use both phases in one workout or repeat either phase for a 41-minute daily workout. The program should be approached with the purpose of proper conditioning; players shouldn't just *ride the bike*.

Teaching Tools and Gimmicks

Why buy something for training purposes when you can make it at home? Here are some of the things you can use in teaching, training, and drilling your players, at little or no cost to you.

Sawed-Off Wooden Bats

Half of the barrel has been shorn off the top two bats illustrated in Figure 8-1. You can use these to teach bunting with the notion of getting *on top of the ball*. With the top half sawed off, a player getting under the ball misses it rather than pops it up.

Figure 8-1

The lower two bats in Figure 8-1 are particularly valuable in teaching the downward approach in hitting. They are short bats cut off right about where the barrel begins. The hitter places one of these bats in the lead hand, or bottom hand, and holds it by the ear with a good *L* position as he kneels before a batting tee, as shown in Figure 8-2. Have him swing with the bottom hand only, drive through the ball on the tee, and finish high. Bring the knob of the bat right down to the hitting zone. Players will build muscle memory for a properly executed swing with these half bats.

Figure 8-2

Paddles

Another device useful in teaching the approach of the hands to the baseball is a simple paddle. You can use ping-pong paddles or even old broken ice hockey goalie sticks (they are a bit more sturdy). Set a whiffle ball on the tee and have the hitter swing at the ball with the paddle. First, they should work their swing using only the bottom hand, and then only the top hand.

Lax-bat

As for teaching the art of bunting, this one seems to be one of the best: a wooden bat sawed off and drilled with a lacrosse stick attached to the top, as shown in Figure 8-3. Players can literally *catch* the ball.

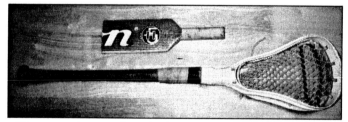

Figure 8-3. Players can learn to bunt by hitting with a combined bat/lacrosse stick.

Paddle Gloves

Without doubt, these are great teaching devices. You can make them from quarter-inch plywood with cotton work gloves, as shown in Figure 8-4. Staple the gloves to the back of the plywood with a thin piece of old blanket or rug remnant affixed between the glove and the wood to serve as padding. You can also create paddle gloves from old football thigh pads and belts, as illustrated in Figure 8-5. Wall drills, crossover exchange tosses, double-play pivot drills, etc., all utilize these practically cost-free yet priceless paddle gloves.

Figure 8-4. Paddle gloves made with plywood and work gloves

Figure 8-5. Paddle gloves made with football pads and belts

Sand-Filled Tennis Can

Fill tennis cans with sand and use them as part of a program to strengthen the throwing arm (as described in Chapter 4).

Target Tire

The target tire is mounted on a slab of wood about two feet by six feet as illustrated in Figure 8-6. This setup offers much flexibility as a workstation. It can be placed atop a box or old chair to establish the proper height for pitchers to hone their accuracy skills. Other suggestions are to mount one on a backstop or swing one from a tree limb with rope.

Figure 8-6. Target tire

Towel Drills

Use old towels or rags for this series of drills to strengthen the arms. Have your pitchers hold the towel in the pitching hand and throw through their range of motion in an attempt to snap the towel like a whip. This teaches them to snap the wrist at the release of the ball.

Other towel drills include isotonic exercises such as a second player holding the other end of the towel while the working player goes through his throwing motion or the motion of the lead arm in hitting, as his teammate provides mild resistance. For the isotonic drills, surgical tubing is a good replacement for the towel.

Surgical Tubing

Tubing can be purchased at any medical supply store. Attach it to the backstop for arm-strengthening drills.

Eggs

Have you got a team with hands of stone? If they don't know how to give with the ball and soften their hands, bring in a carton of eggs and make them play catch. Drilling with eggs also teaches them to get their hands out in front of their bodies and *look the ball in*. Even with gloves on, broken eggs don't harm the leather—and you'll certainly get their attention!

Tape Balls

Never throw out old battered baseballs. Rip off the cover and tape them up with athletic tape. You can use these recycled balls in the pitching machine, off the batting tee, or in soft-toss drills.

Box Targets

Keep a couple of fair-sized cardboard boxes or plastic milk crates around to use as targets in bunting contests. Place the boxes on the field and have players practice bunting the ball into each box.

Netting

Never throw away netting; it's worth its weight in gold to a baseball coach. You can always think up a new drill station as long as you have netting. For example, open the doors to the gym or storage shed and suspend a section of netting from it to create a ball-toss station.

Wooden L Screens

Why spend money on a protective screen for batting practice when you can make one? (This is another use for your old netting.) Figure 8-7 illustrates the specifications, although you can build one to suit your own needs. Make sure to set two 2x4 or 2x6 balances across the base to keep the screen upright. After you've built the frame, drape netting over it and use a staple gun to secure the netting.

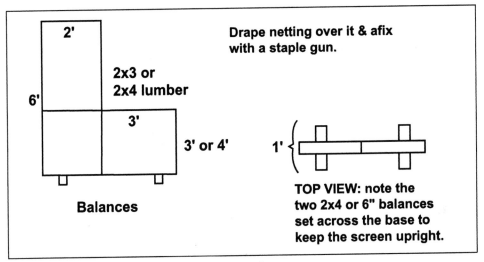

Figure 8-7. Wooden "L" screen for batting practice

Bats and Balls with Eyelets

Drill an eyelet into a bat or ball, as illustrated in Figures 8-8 and 8-9, and attach it to surgical tubing, or even to a piece of rope. This helps to provide resistance through the range of motion that develops strength. You may even wish to suspend a ball from a backstop yardarm as a hanging batting tee, as shown in Figure 8-10. Or, attach a ball to the end of a 10-foot rope. Swing it around and have the batter work on hitting the curve ball. Have the twirler make the ball rise and fall to give the batter practice at hitting the two-plane breaking pitch.

Figure 8-8

Figure 8-9

Figure 8-10   Figure 8-11

Upright-Ball Bucket

This simple and easy-to-make tool saves wear and tear on the coach during pitching-batting practice because he doesn't have to bend over to pick up the balls. To make an upright ball bucket, procure a milk crate and cut holes in all four corners. Insert two-by three-inch studs for the legs. Frame them and screw them into a plastic ball crate as illustrated in Figure 8-11.

By using these tools and other *gimmicks*, as well as ones you devise yourself, you can keep your kids more focused in practice and your workouts more lively while keeping costs down. You can establish more drill stations with imagination and creativity that will translate to more teaching and repetitions.

Suggestions for Off-Season Development

At the end of the each season, you should conduct individual meetings with every player. You should always offer a formula for skill and strength development your players can use during the off-season. In addition to a weight-training program (such as the one described in the next section), you may want to suggest the following:

- Attend a camp.
- Regularly visit the batting cages.
- Do wall drills.
- Practice batting from a tee.

- Practice throwing through a tire for pitching accuracy.

- Get a family member or friend to hit fungoes to you.

- Practice quickness starts from a lead-steal position.

You may wish to give players a preseason-conditioning program so they can prepare for the next season in advance:

- Run a mile every other day.

- Do strength training and speed work on the days you don't run.

- Throw and catch on days you don't do weight training.

- Run bleacher steps for speed work.

- Practice quickness starts from a lead-steal position (15 feet).

- Practice quickness starts backtracking on fly balls (10 to 30 yards).

Each of the last three drills needs 10 to 20 reps.

Putting it all together, it may look like this:

- Monday, Wednesday, Friday: Weight training and speed work (weight train first).

- Tuesday, Thursday, Saturday: Distance running and throwing.

- Sunday: Rest.

Keep in mind that an effective training program—conditioning or strength-oriented—takes about six weeks to produce results.

Weight Training for Baseball

The weight-training program described in this section is intended for players of high school age, and may not be appropriate for younger players with underdeveloped muscles. The program is designed to enhance muscular development for strength and endurance; it's not intended for bulk and size. Players need to warm up prior to lifting and stretch afterwards. Workouts should occur three days per week during the off-season and two days during the season for maintenance. Avoid training 36 hours before a game; try to work out after games.

- Bench press: 3 sets of 10 repetitions each

- Three-quarter squats: 3 sets of 10 repetitions (See Figure 8-12.)

Three-quarter squats call for the lifter to squat down to a point where the bottom of the thigh is parallel to the ground—no full squats as in power lifting. Some coaches may yet advocate full squats, but consider this: is there any athletic movement in baseball that calls for knees bent at a greater angle than 90 degrees? Note in Figure 8-12 that the area directly behind the knee and on the underbelly of the thigh is parallel to the ground. This is the desired depth of the squat.

Figure 8-12. Three-quarter squats

- Dumbbell standing flies: 2 sets of 10 repetitions (See Figure 8-13.) The front deltoid lift, shown in Figure 8-14, can be substituted for the standing flies. Make sure to lift up and twist the thumb down to work the rotator cuff in the front deltoid lift.

Figure 8-13. Dumbbell standing flies

Figure 8-14. Front deltoid lift

170

- Dumbbell chest circles: 2 sets of 10 repetitions (See Figure 8-15.) Rotate the dumbells up and around in large circles.

Figure 8-15. Dumbbell chest circles

- Lead (batting) arm reverse curls: 2 sets of 10 repetitions (See Figure 8-16.)

Figure 8-16. Lead-arm reverse curls

- Wrist roller: 2 to 4 repetitions rolling up, 2 to 4 repetitions rolling down. Use a five- to ten-pound weight plate at the end of a rope, as shown in Figure 8-17.

Figure 8-17. Wrist roller

- Trunk twist: 100 to 300 reps
- Prone triceps extensions (pullovers): 2 sets of 10 repetitions (See Figure 8-18.)

Figure 8-18. Prone triceps extensions

- Seated triceps extensions: 2 sets of 10 repetitions (See Figure 8-19.) Two variations are shown.

Figure 8-19. Seated triceps extensions

On off days, throw a football and/or work out with surgical tubing. Add sit-ups as well as stretching and running.

This program is recommended for high school and college athletes. Younger players can do a lighter version of the program, including the use of the surgical tubing and tennis can exercises, or throwing a football to enhance strength in the throwing arm.

Baseball players are advised to refrain from bicep curls—they are of no value in baseball. The reason is that baseball's kinesthetics involve arm extension motions almost exclusively. Triceps are used—not biceps. Curls develop the biceps, which actually serve as the antagonistic muscles for the triceps.

Wrist Curls

When coaches refer to weight-training exercises to strengthen the wrists, they're actually referring to the surrounding muscles. Wrists are joints that cannot be strengthened in and of themselves, but the muscles involved in support and stabilization can be enhanced through even modest weight training.

Wrist Curl Exercise #1

Resting a light dumbbell on the thigh, pull the weight up and down through the full range of motion. See Figure 8-20.

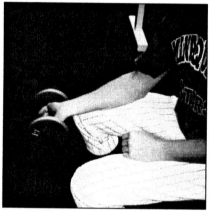

Figure 8-20

Wrist Curl Exercise #2

Again resting the dumbbell, turn it over to both sides in supination and pronation. See Figure 8-21.

Figure 8-21

Wrist Curl Exercise #3

Hold a bat at the base of the handle. Tilt it outward and then back toward your face.

Replicate, turning over the wrist as in a curve ball action. See Figure 8-22.

Figure 8-22

Wrist Curl Exercise #4

Hold a bat in the throwing hand and replicate a slider's hand-and-wrist motion by turning the bat out and away from your body at a 45-degree angle. See Figure 8-23.

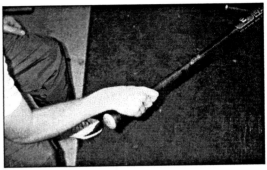

Figure 8-23

Repeat each exercise in 10 to 15 sets of 15 to 20 reps. This series also strengthens the forearm muscles used in all of baseball.

Drills

Always use drills that are relevant to what you're teaching your players. As obvious as this sounds, many coaches implement a drill just because it looks like a good drill. Ask yourself if a particular drill is either a teaching drill that only needs to be done once, or a conditioning or agility drill which needs to be done regularly and repetitively. Once your system is in place, check whether your drills cover elements of the game your team is having trouble with. In other words, are you correcting mistakes with your drills? Each drill needs to serve a purpose and have a focus.

Basic Throwing Drills

These drills are especially valuable in baseball or softball camps, but they need to be incorporated in youth ball, too. Do them as part of your daily warm-up and prepractice routine.

Foot-Plant Drill

To develop good upper-body rotation, have the players throw without allowing a step toward the target. Both feet should face the target and be planted about shoulder width apart, as Figure 8-24 illustrates.

Figure 8-24. Foot-plant drill

Follow-Through Drill

Have the players drop to one knee—the one on their throwing-hand side. From this position they throw with their elbow raised to shoulder level (as shown in Figure 8-25), moving the arm diagonally across the chest, ending up by touching the ground on the glove-hand side. A variation is to have the players turn to the side so that their glove-hand side faces the target. This forces them to seek good upper-body rotation.

Figure 8-25. Follow-through drill

Wrist-Snap Drill with Elbow Up

Players start by positioning the elbow of their throwing hand in line with the shoulder; the throwing hand should be at a right angle to the bicep of the upper arm. Then have them throw using an abbreviated motion with the lower arm, and end by snapping the wrist to complete the throw.

Crow-Hop Drill

Teach them proper form: with the foot on the throwing-hand side, step and turn the toe out away from the body, and then execute. Upper-body turn and weight distribution onto the back pivot foot are essential.

Two-Hands Drill

Have the players close their gloves and catch the ball with the back of their mitts to ensure a two-handed catch. For safety's sake, and to keep proper form for the drill, remind any players who have a glove with an outside finger loop to place their fingers—all of them—inside the mitt.

Specialized Positional Throwing Drills

Pitchers

Two excellent drills for pitchers include:

- Without a baseball, have a pitcher come to the *tuck* position, balancing on one leg with the stride leg raised prior to breaking for home plate. Have him hold that position because balance is so critical in pitching mechanics. Then flip him a ball and have him release and follow-through toward home with a well-thrown pitch.

- Set the pitcher's trail leg—or the one he pushes off the rubber with—on a chair, as shown in Figure 8-26. Use the bleachers if you want to drill the pitchers en masse. Have them assume a stride-out position with the stride-leg toe facing home and their chest rotated homeward, too. The throwing arm should be cocked with the elbow at shoulder level. Now they throw and follow through properly. Emphasize bending the back in this drill.

Figure 8-26. Chair drill for pitchers

Catchers

The throw-from-the-knees drill and the footwork drill presented in the section on coaching catchers in Chapter 7 are also part of this category.

Dominican Throwing Drills

Players coming from the Dominican Republic are proliferating in the big leagues now, and they're all excellent ball players. Why? Not only do they play baseball year-round, but they also emphasize things that most coaches in the United States don't. They develop more fluidity and flexibility in their training, instead of emphasizing speed, power, and size. The following are infield throwing drills done in the Dominican Republic (as discussed by Jim Lefebvre in a coaching clinic):

Prone Throwing

To teach the snap throw, have the infielders lie on their backs and toss a ball up in the air to themselves. The arm begins above the shoulder and points to the sky on the follow-through.

Four-Man Flip-and-Throw

Four players stand as shown in Figure 8-27, with two sets of two players facing each other. One player flips a ball to his partner, who catches it barehanded and throws to the distant set of partners. There are no stops in the flow of the flip-and-throw; the drill should emphasize fluidity. The second pair of players replicates the drill and throws the ball back.

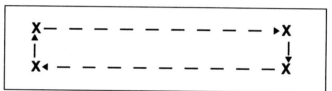

Figure 8-27. Four-man flip-and-throw

One-Leg Balance Throws

Have players throw sidearm or underhand off one leg, balanced on their throwing-side leg.

Softball Throws

Throwing a softball can develop arm strength. Also, high school coaches who teach the split-finger sinker use a softball to spread the index and forefinger. (Be careful, as some coaches feel that the split-finger pitch creates arm trouble.)

Line Drills

These can easily be incorporated into your daily throwing drills. Set the players up in two parallel lines as illustrated in Figure 8-28, just as if they were having a regular catch. Besides crow-hops, stationary foot-planted throwing, two-hand back-of-the-glove catches, and others described earlier, work these quick drills:

- Lateral crossovers with balls rolled side-to-side—also known as *pick-ups*, this drill is an old standby.
- Backhanding: Players roll the ball to their partner's backhand for proper form.
- Paddle gloves: Use for both grounders and quick-return throws.
- Shovel feeds: Have the players face upfield with their glove-hand sides facing each other so they can work shovel feeds. This is an effective teaching tool for infielders.

You can also set the players in squares about 25 feet apart to work many of these same drills.

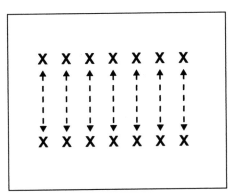

Figure 8-28

The box drill can also be very effective in teaching footwork such as shuffle-steps and hop-turns. Line up three or four players at each corner, as illustrated in Figure 8-29. Have them catch and throw employing proper quickness and fluidity, and then follow-up their throw by rotating to the end of the line at the next corner.

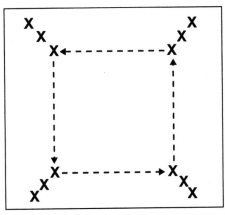

Figure 8-29. Box drill

Wall Drills

Align players facing a building or gymnasium wall 6 to 10 feet away. They can use paddle gloves or their own mitts. Use old beat up baseballs for this set of drills.

- Drill 1: Throw the ball against the wall and work on proper ground ball fielding form. Encourage soft hands.

- Drill 2: Set a player close to the wall, perhaps six feet away. Set another player behind him. This second player throws a crisp one-hop ball over the shoulder of the player in front, who must field it.

- Drill 3: Set the players facing at right angles to the wall with their glove side nearest the wall. Have them work on the shovel-feed throw and then square up to field the ball.

Specialized Hitting Drills

Short-Toss Batting Practice

Place an L screen about 15 to 20 feet from the batter and with a short, dart-throwing motion, toss balls on the outside half of the plate so that he must drive the ball to the opposite field. The coach serving as pitcher should be seated behind the screen.

Double-Tee Batting Drills

The following three drills use two tees placed side by side.

Drill #1: Hitting the Inside Pitch

Facing a pitcher who works the ball inside (and there aren't that many who do), a hitter may end up getting *sawed off* on the bat handle or pulling off the ball and the plate in feeble efforts to adjust. You should teach hitters to drive the ball hard by adjusting the approach of the bottom hand. This hand takes you to the ball, and it must take more of an inside route on an inside pitch. As obvious as that sounds, it's difficult for hitters to comply with unless they've practiced— hence the double tee (shown in Figure 8-30). The inside tee provides a ball to hit and the outside one that's set taller serves as a block against a swing that's too looping and extended. If the batter hits the distant tee, then he must keep his hands more inside.

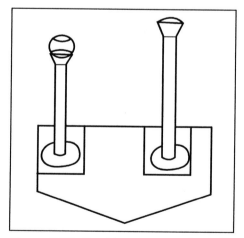

Figure 8-30. Double tee setup for Drills #1 and #2

Drill #2: The Called Swing

Use the same double-tee setup you used for Drill #1. In Drill #2, teach the hitter to adjust his bottom hand approach inside or out depending upon pitch location. On the commands *trigger* and *stride*, the hitter attacks either tee. Both are loaded with a ball—one inside and one outside. The coach's command of *in* or *out* provides the adjustment key after the hitter has set his weight back. The hitter must trust his hands after striding and keep his hands and weight back. After one ball is hit, have the batter simply hit the other ball with no call, while still practicing good mechanics.

Drill #3: High-Low Tees

To teach the downward approach of the bat head, set one tee atop home plate and another without a ball directly behind it and taller. The batter must drive the ball off the front tee without striking the back tee. In Figure 8-31, home plate is shown from the side. The arrow indicates the route of the bat swing.

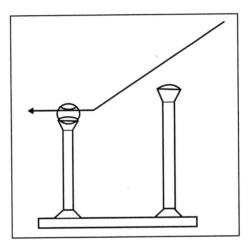

Figure 8-31. High-low tees

Rhythm Hitting off a Tee

Set the batter in a good, balanced stance addressing a batting tee. Gripping the bat with both hands, he swings the bat across the body and toward an imaginary pitcher. Then, in a continuous motion, he returns to his original stance, holing the bat high and placing his weight fluidly on the back foot. Rhythm is the key word.

Golf Ball Batting Practice

Buy a bag of whiffle-style golf balls. Use a cut off broomstick handle for a bat. Short toss the balls from behind a pitching screen and see how the hitters learn to control their swing and focus their visual targeting. You should be advised that a well hit ball driven sharply back at you can raise a welt, so make sure to *chuck and duck*!

Odd-Angle Ball Toss

Instead of the conventional ball-toss drills from the side of the hitter, try soft-tossing from behind the batter (they learn to track the ball better and quicken their hands), or dropping the ball from atop the strike/hitting zone (call for stride, trigger, and then drop it). They should be hitting into a net, a fence, or a screen. This drill is innovative, different, and challenging for hitters.

Called Sequences

Once you've taught the proper mechanics of hitting and pitching, take your players through their technical sequences with verbal calls. Break down each step of the motion and have them freeze at each call. This is an effective method of instruction that builds muscle memory and teaches key words for you to use during live action. Have the hitters work off a batting tee with the pitchers on a mound—or you can line up along a foul line for mass instruction. For example, a call sequence for hitters might be:

- Weight back   • Stride

- Trigger   • Swing

    For your pitchers, the calls might be:

- Take the sign   • Break and stride

- Rocker step   • Deliver

- Pivot foot   • Follow through

- Turn and tuck

    Be careful not to overuse this staccato technique, as it does break up a motion that should be fluid.

Rundown Drill

For the rundown drill, divide the players into groups of three, including the outfielders. Begin with a runner trapped in the middle between two bases, as shown in Figure 8-32. On the whistle, initiate the drill's movement with a throw from the base he came from. This allows the player guarding the lead base to run the player back. For groups who don't have a true baseline to work on, simply designate which is the lead base. For example, make the first baseline and foul line the back base, with the baseline between second and third the upfield or lead base. Rotate all three people after two to three rundowns.

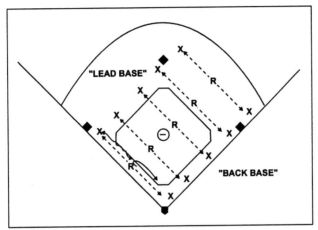

Figure 8-32. Rundown drill

Coaching points:

- Hold the ball high so everybody can see it.
- Always run the player back to the base he came from.
- You're allowed one pump fake; use it only when you have eye contact with the runner.
- Be under control as you run the trapped runner back.
- When the runner gets within a body length of the base, snap the throw to the receiver for a sweep tag (generally about five to seven feet away from the base).

Relay and Cutoff Drills

Drill #1

The first drill involves teaching the techniques of relay throws. Line up all the infielders in a straight line, with at least 30 feet between players—it may run the entire length of your field complex. Begin with a single ball at one end of the line. The players relay the ball down the line utilizing these proper techniques:

- Raise two hands in the air to signal for the throw.
- Use two hands for a quick catch and release.

- Catch the ball across the body (i.e., turn once the ball is launched) so the fielder merely has to catch, step, and throw, all in one fluid motion. As a coaching point, remember that the glove-side should be toward the target.
- Throw the ball at the target's chest or head.

Drill #2

In the second drill, illustrated in Figure 8-33, station your fielders in positions simulating a game situation and spray fungoed base hits everywhere. For each hit, there's a runner on second who tries to stretch it and race for home. Have him challenge the fielders. You can make a game out of this drill by seeing how many outs are made versus how many runs are scored. Tell the runner to be overly aggressive so you can work live rundowns.

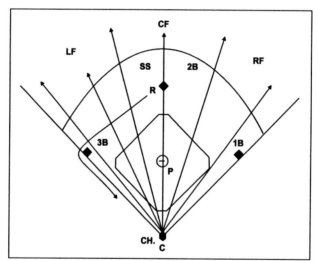

Figure 8-33. Relay-and-cutoff drill #2

Infield-Coordination Drills

Drill #1

Pitchers are infielders—although they sometimes forget that. This drill helps instill a sense of involvement as well as coordinate their movements and reactions with the other infielders.

Line up the pitchers by the mound as shown in Figure 8-34, and set your infielders at their positions. Fungo a series of balls to the right side and then to the left side. Work on throws to first, covering first; throws to second base, slow-rollers to both sides of the mound, and calls and combination plays with the first and third basemen.

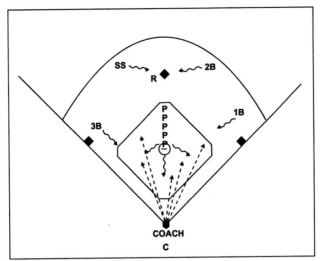

Figure 8-34. Infield-coordination drill #1

Involve catchers in this drill emphasizing footwork, rounding the ball so that their glove-side shoulder points to the base they intend to throw to, and using two hands to field the ball. Work your left-side infield combinations, too, so that third basemen and shortstops coordinate their reads on a slow-roller with the third baseman cutting across the shortstop's path on a play to first.

Drill #2

This teaching drill only needs to be done once in preseason. Set your infielders at their positions with their backups waiting in foul territory ready to jump in. Start with a fungo and a play to first. After that, everything emanates from calls. Since every base should be covered, the coach yells out, "Two," or "Four," or "Three," in random sequence. Players throw to the called base. Continue until 10 consecutive, flawless throws are made, or until there's an error, and then the second unit races on to the field.

Drill #3

The two-ball infield pregame warm-up described in Chapter 2 should be used here, and you can use it as a drill in practice, too.

Crossfire Infield Drill

Most coaches believe in the value of repetition, so use this drill to maximize the number of ground balls your infielders get during a practice. Divide your infielders into groups of four, then have them pair off and line up as shown in Figure 8-35. One player fungoes grounders while another feeds him. Another player fields them, and yet another backs up the fielder (the latter is expendable if you don't have enough players). Each group gets a bat and four balls.

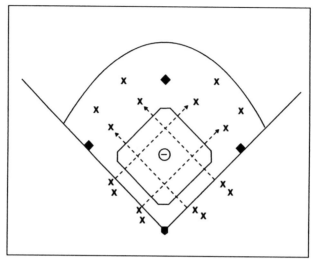

Figure 8-35. Crossfire infield drill

Once alignments are set, the crossfire of fungoed grounders begins. In three or four minutes, infielders should receive up to 25 grounders each. Rotate players by having the hitter become the feeder and the fielder go to backup duty—then rotate both groups. Use a whistle to signal rotations.

Don't allow players to chase a muffed ball as collisions can result. Also, they must never chase a short-hit ball lying on the infield grass. If you've provided at least four baseballs, that should be plenty to keep the drill moving. If you want to really work a player or shake things up a bit, you hit the fungoes instead of a player.

Since it is your outfielders who are hitting the fungoes in this drill, why not reverse it and have the infielders hit to the outfield? Set them in groups in left field, center, and right. Besides lazy fly balls, hit gappers coordinating two groups at once, and then work sliding catches on Texas-Leaguers, as well as backtracking on balls hit over their heads. In each situation, use a cutoff man. You will need three fungo teams for this drill, all positioned in the infield.

Infield-Corners Drill

This drill provides work on your infielders' key throws:

- Sequence #1: Middle infielders work on double-play pivots with throws snapped to a first baseman two-thirds of the way back toward first base. First and third basemen work on bunts and slow rollers to each other. (Refer to Figure 8-36.)

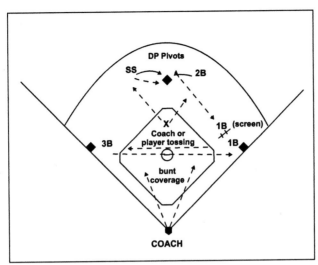

Figure 8-36. Infield-corners drill, sequence #1

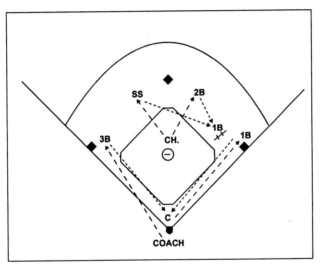

Figure 8-37. Infield-corners drill, sequence #2

- Sequence #2: Middle infielders work on their throws to first in the same alignment as shown in sequence 1 (with a first baseman set two-thirds of the way down the line). Provide a screen to protect the other first basemen. The first and third basemen practice their throws to the plate with a live catcher who works on curling down to apply the tag. (Refer to Figure 8-37.)

- Sequence #3: Finish the drill with middle infielders throwing to the plate, while first and third basemen work on the mechanics of their relay throws to the plate by receiving throws from either an outfielder or another infielder stationed up the foul line. Coaches need to direct traffic on this sequence using a whistle. (Refer to Figure 8-38.)

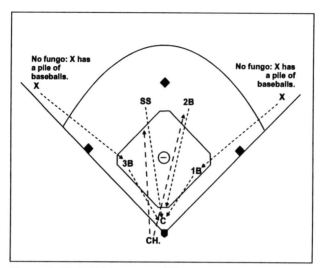

Figure 8-38. Infield-corners drill, sequence #3

Drill for Holding Runners and Working Pickoff Throws

Group your pitchers by the mound and work three at a time. As illustrated in Figure 8-39, one pitcher works on his sequence of moves and throws to first, while another works on his spin move to second, and yet a third works on his throw to third base. You should teach right-handers the same move you teach lefties to first base, and encourage the right-handers to use it over to third, especially on fields with close fences along the left-side foul lines.

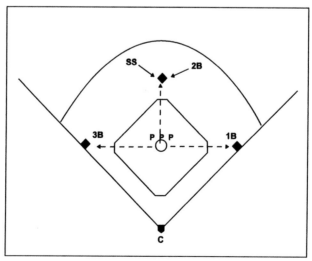

Figure 8-39. Pitcher's pickoff

Enhance teamwork and coordination by having the proper infield position receive the throw. This is especially true for the catcher as his signals need to be coordinated with the pitcher and middle infielders on the spin-move pickoff at second base.

The pitcher throwing to third need not focus entirely there. Have him work pitchouts to the catcher—an often-overlooked component of holding runners. The coaching point on a pitchout is this: have your pitcher focus on a spot on the backstop, not the catcher's glove.

AFTERWORD

In many ways this book represents a milestone in my personal and professional life. I recently turned fifty, saw the birth of my first grandchild, was hired onto the staff of a college baseball team, and finally finished this book after so many years of working on it. Perhaps all that allows me the presumptuous luxury of passing along one final word of advice: don't forget to coach your own kids.

For the professional coach—as opposed to the *Little League Dad* who's in it only for his own child's betterment—you may find that you miss a lot of your own child's successes because of your commitment to all of the kids in your program. Besides quietly watching my daughters in softball or my son in Little League and ice hockey, my fondest memories as a father are the Sunday night practices with Dad. I would never insist, but if they wanted me to pitch a round or two of batting practice in the high school batting cage, or fungo some balls to them, I would leap at the chance. My oldest daughter, Abigail, played varsity softball, and whenever she went into a slump at the plate, she'd ask for a Sunday night practice. Abigail still maintains that her batting average increased after those practices together. For any coach/father there can be no greater reward.

Coach your team with passion, but never forget to coach your *main team*—your family team—with equal if not greater desire. Demonstrate your love of the game through both teams.

ABOUT THE AUTHOR

Dr. Richard Trimble is an assistant baseball coach at Ocean County College in Toms River, New Jersey. He has been on the staff of the Brookdale Baseball Camp for more than 20 years and now directs his own instructional camps, Baseball Prep. Since 1997, he has been the bull pen coach for the Jersey Shore team in the prestigious Carpenter Cup.

Trimble has been coaching baseball since he was 15 years old. After serving as a junior varsity and varsity assistant at two high schools, he moved into the middle school ranks at Manasquan Elementary and Spring Lake Heights schools in New Jersey. His junior varsity teams won more than 100 games, and his middle school record was 118-35-3, including eight conference championships in 14 years. He also coaches ice hockey and has published two drill books for hockey coaches.

Trimble holds five college degrees, including a Ph.D. in American History. He is the author of four previous books. He has taught history at both Manasquan and Monsignor Donovan High Schools, as well as Brookdale Community College, and was honored as the Monmouth County Teacher of the Year in 1995.

Trimble and his wife, Jean, have three children, Abigail, Jill, and Andrew. The family resides in Manasquan, New Jersey.